GIANT KILLERS

OVERCOME THE GIANTS THAT ROB YOU OF YOUR BEST LIFE

TIM HALL

Ark House Press
PO Box 1722, Port Orchard, WA 98366 USA
PO Box 1321, Mona Vale NSW 1660 Australia
PO Box 318 334, West Harbour, Auckland 0661 New Zealand
arkhousepress.com

© 2016 Tim Hall

Cataloguing in Publication Data:
Author: Hall, Tim.
Title: Giant Killers : overcome the giant that robs your best life/Tim Hall.
ISBN: 9781921589485 (pbk.)
Subjects: Christian life--Biblical teaching.
Self-actualization (Psychology)--Religious aspects--Christianity.
Problem solving--Religious aspects--Christianity.
Giants in the Bible.
Dewey Number: 248.4

Cover design by Brandwave
Layout by initiateagency.com
www.initiatemedia.net

Dedication & Acknowledgements

I dedicate this book to my lovely wife Jacquelyn for teaching me what it means by this scripture, "let us consider one another to provoke to love and to good works" (especially book writing), Hebrews 10:24 (American King James Version) and Kevin Charles (Pro Hart) and his dear wife Raylee for the tremendous support of so many of our global campaigns.

I would like to acknowledge Cornelia (Nelly) Farnik for the many hours that she has laboured with us in producing this book.
I would also like to acknowldege Chris Donald (a well published author) who encouraged me for years and then edited this book.

ENDORSEMENTS

Having known Tim Hall over the years, he has always had a passion to see people know victory in their lives through the power of the Holy Spirit and the Word of God. 'Giant Killers' will inspire and motivate you to stand strong in the grace of God through every season of your life.

With much love **Darlene Zschech**

Tim Hall is a dynamic evangelist who has a passion to see souls saved and lives changed by the power of the Holy Spirit. He travels around the world, teaching and preaching and has seen the miraculous power of God impact and transform many lives. Tim's teachings will encourage and inspire you that with God's help, anything is possible.

Brian Houston, Senior Pastor, Hillsong Church

If anyone can speak with complete authority about slaying giants, certainly Tim Hall can. Over the many years of friendship I have enjoyed with this great man of God I have seen him overcome so many immense challenges, all the time carrying an exuberance and joy for life that many don't have even when life's great! We've been blessed so many times in our church and our movement by the giant slaying ministry of Tim Hall. I know this book will empower you to live your life, ruling in your world, through the power of Christ.

Phil Pringle, Senior Minister - Christian City Church Oxford Falls and President of C3 Global

Tim Hall's book 'Giant Killers' is a parallel story of the life of David as he took on Goliath & defeated him, and the everyday believer as they take on the Giants of life. This book written by the hand of a great artist it will paint the picture on the inside of you, of you standing holding the head of the Giant that has harassed and threatened you. Tim Hall one of the leading Evangelist of our Day, a great Australian Artist, an Australian Legend, a man who loves people, loves God with all his heart, my dear & special friend, and brother, Tim we love you dearly.

Dr Rodney M Howard-Browne, Tampa Florida

Tim Hall has been someone who has defeated and overcome Goliaths in his life. This book not only will empower you to overcome giants in your own life but it will also give you the testimony of a life that has actually lived this book, so God can do it again in your life and others. We all face giants of some kind in our lives so I truly believe this book is a must read, it will inspire, motivate and will change your life.

Russell Evans (Founder & Director of Planetshakers)

TABLE OF CONTENTS

INTRODUCTION

A GIANT'S CORPSE
MAKES A GREAT STEPPING STONE

*"Therefore David ran, and stood upon the Philistine,
and took his sword, and drew it out of the sheath
thereof, and slew him, and cut off his head therewith.
And when the Philistines saw their champion was
dead, they fled."* I Samuel 17:51

The motionless form of the giant of Gath lay face down on the battlefield of Shochoh and blood from his forehead seeped into the earth below his face. The great intimidator Goliath, champion of Philistia, lay motionless. His terrifying words had ceased. A smooth stone from a shepherd boy's sling was embedded in his skull. Goliath was finished.

The two armies had stood in silent, stunned amazement and watched the scene play out before them. All eyes were upon the young shepherd boy, whose skill and daring had taken their breath away. He ran towards the massive, armoured, prostrate figure that had stood as the ultimate statement of Philistia's supremacy. In the blink of an eye, history changed.

The young shepherd boy stepped up onto the giant's body. This was the greatest step he had ever taken. He reached down and pulled the huge sword out of Goliath's scabbard. This great weapon had once glinted in the sun and sent fear through all Israel's ranks.

With all of his might, he raised the massive implement of terror. David brought it down with such force that Goliath's huge head rolled, by its own weight, as his life blood drenched the earth.

David's step up onto the prostrate corpse of Goliath was one of the most profound steps ever taken in human history.

For the shepherd boy David, the step was a giant-sized step into the awesome place of destiny that God had ordained for him. It was a step from obscurity and rejection to kingly dominion, fame and wealth, global and eternal influence. It was a step that was ultimately felt as Messiah took His place in history establishing His Kingdom on Earth.

Like David the shepherd boy, an army of giant killers has been prepared by God for this hour. Often with small flocks and in lonely places of isolation, rejection and insignificance, this body of men, women, boys and girls is receiving its training for the most fruitful, significant time ever planned for world history.

When we talk of the age of the giants, Bible scholars talk of the centuries preceding the great flood, the antediluvian age while others talk of the years of conquest when Israel seized the Promised Land. David and his mighty men confronted giants including Goliath of Gath, the best known giant in history. Greek mythology describes an age of giants and global historical records exist of times of the existence of giant races.

I believe that the great era of giants, who oppose our destiny, the Body of Christ globally and the future of all mankind, has come right now in the 21st Century. Like a great sleeping army, giants in so many forms are rising up to confront a formidable Church that is marching with a new purposeful intensity and clothing of divine power.

All through the world, Christians are preparing to take giant steps onto the prostrate corpses of massive, intimidating opponents of destiny. These are giants sent to halt the progress of the Church and bring the world under Satan's control.

Giants are rising up across the earth like never before in human history. They are rising with a sinister purpose in the realms of politics, finance, religion and inexplicable hostilities. There has never been an age in history when giants have stood up like this all across the globe.

It is very evident that the focus of so many giants is the Body of Christ. Their aim is to render the 21st Century Church impotent.

In Zechariah 12:8, we read that in the last days as the world confronts Israel even the feeblest among them will be as David. This, I believe, is the case for the Church, the rise of the giants will see men like David standing up under the mighty hand of God.

What an incredible time to have been called of God. What a day of opportunity!

Like David of old you are about to face giants and see them prostrate before you.

The giants you face are your stepping stones to the awesome place of destiny that God has prepared for you. These great, intimidating, roaring influences that seek your peace, confidence, destiny and inheritance are about to fall face down on your field of battle. You are a giant killer. You were born with destiny and greatness branded like fire into your spirit. Your journey to Kingdom fulfilment will reveal many key stepping stones. Often these stepping stones take the form of giant obstacles of resistance that are forged in Hell to stifle and halt your progress and render you ineffective or destroyed. Each, however; is a God given opportunity to step up to a new place of impact and authority. Each one presents an opportunity to enter a greater position of stature and spiritual authority.

Some years ago I heard Rick Godwin preach a sermon that inspired me to study the giant killers in scripture. One term that he used that stayed in my mind was the following:

"Giants are the breakfast of champions."

He referred to the statement made so many centuries ago by the aged giant killer Caleb when he declared that the giants faced by Israel would be "bread"[1] to them.

---

1   Numbers 14:9

The giants we face are not going to destroy us. We are not their prey. They are ours. They are food for us. They are to be swallowed up by God's anointed champions, by the mighty power indwelling us. They are "our breakfast", strengthening our resolve to step up to each new day. They are health food and stepping stones on our journey to that awesome moment when Jesus declares:

"…Well done good and faithful servant;…"

Matthew 25:23

1
GIANTS

YOU WILL BE CONFRONTED BY THEM

"The spirits of the giants shall be like clouds that shall oppress, corrupt, fall, contend and bruise upon the earth."[1]
"You will be known for the giant you defeat or the giant that defeats you."[2]

Sheets of rain poured down on this dark night in the Highlands of Papua New Guinea. I was a young and enthusiastic evangelist, hungry for the demonstration of God's power. This particular night I preached to a crowd of vibrant people crammed into a large auditorium. They were packed in so tightly as to cause considerable anxiety to the local Fire Department's by-laws. Outside, a huge crowd stood in the rain and listened intently to the word I preached and then experienced His mighty healing touch. For over an hour, people came to the platform, many in wringing wet clothes, to testify to God's miracle power experienced in their bodies. I had not seen such excitement nor heard so many thrilling testimonies in my time of ministry. The power of God had been overwhelming. I marvelled that, in pouring rain, thousands of people had stood outside unwilling to leave. It was a night of personal exhilaration.

I wondered if this would be the commencement of the God-given dreams that had flooded my soul and driven me alone with God for weeks at a time into outback regions of South Australia.

1   Book of Enoch, Charles Knibb, Ethiopian Version
2   Unknown

As I looked through the barred windows of my Highland hotel late that night, I felt a deep satisfaction. It was a feeling of holy accomplishment like never before. It seemed that on this dark, rainy night something had commenced. It seemed my feet had stepped onto the edge of the Promised Land of my dreams and visions. I could see, with the eye of faith, stadiums filled with great seas of humanity. I could see the beaming faces of people, throwing down crutches, sticks and stepping out of wheelchairs. My heart was filled with a great anticipation.

Within a few days I would be on the island of New Britain in Papua New Guinea and preaching at my first mass campaign to at least 10,000 people. I lay down to sleep that night full of hope. An inspired thrill of holy excitement shuddered through me.

How dramatically things can suddenly change. I didn't know that a great giant was about to rise up against my family. I awoke in the early hours of the morning, sweating profusely and totally filled with inexplicable paranoia. I paced about the room, troubled deeply, anxious beyond words.

What was happening? Why was I so overwhelmed with fear? Where was the gift of faith that had filled my soul only hours before? Where was the bold declaration of authority that had scattered devils this past night? Where was that great and tangible sense of God that had permeated the auditorium with wave after wave of miracle power? The awesome, sinister sense of an unholy force surrounded me.

All that seemed to fill my mind was a deep awareness that my family was under siege. I felt totally helpless, so far from home, with the knowledge in my spirit that something, grotesque and murderous, had risen as a great Goliath against everything I held dear.

I think I must have experienced the same intimidation felt by the army of Israel when Goliath took the field. Words of fear, doubt and confusion began to flood my mind. They seemed to roar against me with hatred and bitter resolve.

How could I enter into that place where I could become the hunter not the hunted, the intimidator not the intimidated?

SATAN HATES THE ANOINTING OF GOD

He must squirm with horror and rage at the thought that the whole earth will be totally filled and flooded with God's glory. The thought of the Spirit of God being poured out on all flesh and the imminent coming of Christ, in all His splendour and power, has caused the alarms of Hell to urgently sound. It seems the reserves of Hell are coming forth by the multitude to oppose and halt the onslaught of God's great army. I love what Kathryn Kuhlman the great evangelist once said:

> **"You may try to stop the great move of God's Spirit but it will be like trying to stop Niagara Falls with an umbrella."**

Satan hates the anointing of God. It is amazing to think that he was intimately acquainted with it when he walked with God as "the anointed cherub that covereth".

> *"Thou art the anointed cherub that covereth; and I have set thee so: thou wast upon the holy mountain of God; thou hast walked up and down in the midst of the stones of fire."*
> Ezekiel 28:14

It is hard to believe that he was once a guardian of the anointing of God. The coloured stones over his being must have flashed reflected colour through Heaven. It seems likely that he was Heaven's chief musician, with the anointing surging through the "pipes" and "tabrets"[3] that covered him. He was a glorious reflector and guardian of God's splendour. Now he is the great hater of that which had once been entrusted to him. The anointing on your life represents all that he lost as he fell like lightning from Heaven. His envy and hatred of anyone trusted to carry the glory of God must send him into unspeakable rage.

His hatred of the anointing of God on my life seemed to attract his foul opposition like a shark to blood. I was suddenly aware of Satan's

---

3   Ezekiel 28:13

utter hatred of the power of God on a human life. It is little wonder that, after God's instruction to us in Ephesians 6:10 to be strong and filled with the mighty power of God, he then strongly advises us to be fully armoured for battle to stand against all that Satan wants to throw at us.

Immediately after David had been anointed king, the Philistines sought him out. They gathered in the valley of Rephaim (the valley of giants) to oppose his new place of authority and might.

> *"And when the Philistines heard that David was anointed king over all Israel, all the Philistines went up to seek David. And David heard of it, and went out against them."*
> 1 Chronicles 14:8

The giants who are birthed from Hell, economic, moral and political, are rising up against a Church that is finding its kingly dominion.

Immediately after Jesus was mightily impacted by the power of God at His baptism in the Jordan, he confronted the full onslaught of Satan's trials and accusations in the wilderness.

His total stand of strength in the face of Hell's giant saw him enter the wilderness in the "fullness of the Spirit"[4] and exit there to enter into ministry in the "power of the Spirit"[5]. Again, we see that each giant we face and overcome in uncompromised defiance, enables us to step into a greater dimension of boldness and authority.

In Papua New Guinea giant opposition sought me out. I should have taken that as a real compliment. Looking back, I am now aware that powers of darkness had begun to fear me and set out to stop any advance in my life.

When men or women step into a place of kingly dominion or start to move into the Promised Land that God has prepared for them, the giants array themselves to intimidate, to blockade, to discourage and to hinder. The picture of Israel's onslaught into the Promised Land, where they faced and destroyed giants and seized walled, fortified cities, is our example.

4   Luke 4:1
5   Luke 4:14

I had just stepped into my destiny, into an anointing of strength and authority in the realm of miracles. Into this realm, stepped this giant from Hell, totally committed to halt the call of God and stop the flow of miracle power into which I had embarked.

Thank God that:

> *"No weapon that is formed against thee shall prosper; and every tongue that shall rise against thee in judgment thou shalt condemn. This is the heritage of the servants of the LORD, and their righteousness is of me, saith the LORD."* Isaiah 54:17

Thank God that we are "the head and not the tail"[6], and that we are "more than conquerors"[7] in any situation that can confront us.

This was my time to stand immovable and then to advance against everything that rose up against me and to emerge as a hardened, wiser and more desperate Kingdom warrior. Perhaps you are facing giants that seek to discourage and bring you down. You are not one who shrinks back. You are an unstoppable child of God. Truly, no weapon formed against you will prosper.

DEAD GIANTS ARE A STAIRCASE FOR DESTINY

If you desire the miraculous power of God, in your life and ministry, you will step as an anointed gladiator into an arena of faith where giants will seek to utterly destroy you. However, you are stepping in as God's anointed giant killing champion, who will use their huge carcasses as one great staircase to mighty places of impact, influence and success.

The Word of God tells us that had the princes of this world known what Jesus would do, they would never have crucified Him[8]. If the princes (giants) of darkness could possibly know what you will <u>achieve under the</u> mighty hand of God, they would never dare to

6   Deuteronomy 28:13

7   Romans 8:37

8   1 Corinthians 2:8

touch you or confront you. You are God's giant killer raised up even before the foundation of the earth. Giants coming against you are a complimentary statement that a great future lies ahead. They are your "breakfast of champions" and you are destined to swallow them up as you move ever forward.

As I knew that a Goliath had risen against my family, I cancelled my next campaign and flew home to confront and stand ferociously against the giant that had walked onto my field of endeavour.

This giant took me into my darkest seasons of pain as he assaulted my family. For one year I pulled out of ministry and focussed on rebuilding a shattered situation. I entered a season of extended fasting and prayer and gave myself each day to many hours fervently seeking God's face. During the next few years, I had to confront and defeat giants of intimidation, fear, cynicism, discouragement, self doubt and rejection. At times it all seemed too much but now I look back with a certainty that these onslaughts from Hell have injected into my life a sense of resolve, strength and anointing that could have come no other way. I look back now on a trail of dead giants that has been building for our family a staircase for destiny.

GIANTS - SUPERNATURALLY BIRTHED

"That the sons of God saw the daughters of men that they were fair; and they took them wives of all which they chose.
And the Lord said, my spirit shall not always strive with man, for that he also is flesh: yet his days shall be an hundred and twenty years.
There were giants in the earth in those days; and also after that, when the sons of God came in unto the daughters of men, and they bare children to them, the same became mighty men which were of old, men of renown.
And God saw that the wickedness of man was great in the earth, and that every imagination of the thoughts of his heart was only evil continually."
Genesis 6:2-5

The giants we read of in scripture resulted when angels left their abode and involved themselves in illegal sexual union with women of the earth whom they took as wives. The result of the union of angels and humans produced massive and extraordinary races of people. The men became giant, renowned, ruthless warriors who filled the earth with terror.

These giants were supernaturally birthed with devastating and destructive purpose. The giants that oppose your destiny will likewise be supernaturally birthed with a special purpose – to stop, hinder, frustrate and, if possible, destroy you.

These giant races were ruthless and mercilessly intent on destruction. We are totally deceived if we underestimate the purpose and intent of the giants we face on our journey of faith.

ARCHAEOLOGY REVEALS GIANTS ACROSS THE EARTH

Giants appear in ancient writings from across the globe. It is possible that they play a central role in Greek mythology and their existence has been confirmed by archaeological finds across most continents.

Archaeologists uncovered a huge bed in Tutankhamen's tomb in Egypt. It was a massive bed 3½ m (11.5 feet) long by 2 m (6.5 feet) wide and also a 2 metre (6.5 foot) sword. This was almost certainly the bed of a giant bodyguard who was buried alive in the pharaoh's tomb. His non-mummified remains decayed to powder but his bed and sword bear witness to his existence and obvious protective role with Pharaoh. Giants were certainly found in the regions of Egypt and Canaan.

Archaeologists across the USA and many other continents, including Australia, have uncovered mounds and graves with skeletal remains of giants between 3 and 4 m (3.2-4.3 yards) or (10-13 feet) in height. Some of these giants have six fingers and toes and two rows of teeth.

BOOK OF ENOCH

A study of the ancient apocryphal book of Enoch is most interesting. Although this book was not canonised, the early Church accepted it as a valid source of information. The fact that Jude quotes directly from the book declaring Enoch a prophet gives us a reason to research it.

> "And Enoch also, the seventh from Adam, prophesied of these, saying, Behold, the Lord cometh with ten thousands of his saints," Jude 1:14

This book of Enoch gives us insight into the events leading up to the great Genesis flood. It reveals that angels descended to earth because of the beauty of women they saw there and cohabited with them. Enoch gives insight into a human race subjugated by fallen angels and vicious giant offspring who wreaked total havoc on the human race. The horror of the supernatural mixing with the natural realm saw a world cast into utter violent depravity and brought God to a place where He would flood the earth.

The Genesis account lines up clearly with Enoch's words:

> "And God looked upon the earth, and, behold, it was corrupt; for all flesh had corrupted his way upon the earth
> And God said…The end of all flesh is come before me; for the earth is filled with violence through them: and, behold, I will destroy them with the earth."
> Genesis 6:12-13

When men involve themselves with demons, giants are brought to birth. When Christians refuse to put down their pet sins and walk a fine line of spirituality and carnality they are spawning their own giants. Today pornography and every vile thing are available through the internet, movies and magazines. The child of God must cautiously prevent the mixing of the holiness of God and the filth of carnality. The result, like in Genesis chapter 6, is giants. Giants may grow from situations we have let go and not addressed.

Recently, we have been stunned by the tragic fall of a young dynamic preacher with an extraordinary preaching gift. Sadly, a situation in his life had not been addressed by him and, at the time when his ministry was impacting the country, everything fell apart and his incredible impact has ceased. By God's grace, our prayers are that he will again be raised up.

Procrastination allows giants to grow to full stature. There may be giants in our minds that have started as seed thoughts and grown into great strongholds because they were not dealt with early enough.

In the late 1960s, I trained at the South Australian School of Art. One subject that I chose was ceramics (or pottery). The processes involved in working with clay have interesting parallels in life. One great lesson was this. Prior to centring the clay on the pottery wheel, it had to be "wedged". This involved the rolling of the clay upward followed by strong downward pressure of the hands. The clay was again rolled upward followed again by strong downward compression with both hands, much like kneading dough. The process was repeated over and over to remove all the small air bubbles in the clay.

In the heat of the kiln during firing, these small air bubbles, if not dealt with, caused the pots to explode and they often destroyed other pots on shelves around them. These small air bubbles of sin undealt with in people's lives will stay unnoticed till the kiln of life's circumstances (especially ministry) is heated to a high temperature. These small air bubbles become a giant threat to the whole stacked kiln. In the same way, sin undealt with becomes a giant of extreme strength when the heat of ministry and life is greatly increased.

Satan's aim is to produce a giant that can stop you and me. Self examination and a clean walk before God will prevent any giant being raised up within our own character. Sin undealt with creates a cauldron of opportunity for a satanic giant to be raised up within our own lives and family.

Continual prayer, especially with selected intercessors, will also place a protection and a system of warnings around our lives to short circuit satanic methods.

GIANTS ARE FORGED FOR A PURPOSE

The giants faced by Israel aimed to achieve the following:
- To immobilize the Israelites in their minds.
- To strip away their courage.
- To strip away their self-esteem.
- To nullify their purpose.
- To dampen their vision.
- To halt their progress.
- To make their circumstances seem bigger than God.
- By the giants' weight and size, to try to block God out of the picture.
- To make them feel like grasshoppers, mere insects incapable of great things, vulnerable and weak.
- To inhibit and block out their dreams.
- To cause in them double-mindedness, fostering confusion and fear. The giants you face have the same intention.

GIANTS DO OUR HOMEWORK FOR US

The giants we face certainly cause us to examine ourselves.
- They test our resolve.
- Their presence puts a focus on our prayer life.
- They assess our hunger in prayer.
- Their presence establishes whether we have the attitude of Caleb and Joshua to go in and possess the land or if we are like the ten unbelieving spies.
- Their presence either causes us to cringe and hide or to come out onto the field of conflict as anointed warriors.

In the course of history, the greatest pictures of triumph, courage and achievement have generally come in the face of overwhelming giant obstacles. The 300 Spartans, who faced an army of 200,000 Persians, Hannibal of Carthage, who crossed the snowy Alps to bring Rome to her knees, and David the shepherd boy, who brought down the massive Philistine, stir our hearts.

The greatest stories in the Christian world's history will continue to come in future years as giants spawned in Hell fall before God's anointed warriors.

THE GIANTS THAT OPPOSE US HAVE NAMES

Goliath, Arba, Ishbibenob, Og, Sheshai are a few of the names of the giants faced by the giant killers of Scripture. They each had families, weapons and purpose.

The giants we face also have names, relatives, weapons and purpose. They rise up with a clear objective to hinder, halt or prevent our progress into the Promised Land of our own call of God.

The following is a list of some of the giants we can face in our journey of destiny:

- Injustice
- Intimidation
- Fear of death, failure, family loss, phobia of many types, each with its own name.
- Sickness and Disease
- Depression and Despair
- Weight Problems
- Satanic Opposition
- Double mindedness
- Debt
- Shame
- Disappointment
- Addictions
- Betrayal
- Financial Barriers
- Political Roadblocks
- Persecution
- Self Doubt and Insecurities
- Family Tragedies
- Despair

- Low Self Esteem
- Discouragement
- Rejection
- Divorce
- Guilt

Let us look at some of the giants that come against so many saints of God.

DISCOURAGEMENT[9]

The first glance at the name of this giant tells us that his aim is to remove courage.

Discouragement targets your mind with the shadow of defeat. He constantly bellows out words of failure and despair and carries in his hand the sword of depression. He speaks words geared to wear you down and immobilise you. Unfortunately, the giant of discouragement often speaks through those who should be building you up and stirring you to great heights of achievement. He tries to make you withdraw and isolate yourself. He aims to fill you with a great sense of inferiority and causes you to feel of no value.

One favoured weapon of the giant of discouragement is slander or false accusation. The giant may take the form of a business partner, a family member or a doctor's report. It may be constantly bombarding your mind and emotions with defying accusations, threats, doubts and challenges. This giant grows out of past disappointments and is defeated by the giant killer who doesn't know how to give up.

This giant is defeated by the man or woman who just keeps on getting up. Like Rocky Balboa in the movie 'Rocky', discouragement cannot prevail over the man or woman who just keeps standing up on the inside.

---

9   "Discourage – deprived of the will to persist in something." · Collins Pocket Dictionary, p143

Some years ago, a lady from our church went through trauma that would destroy most people. Her son and his friend were working under a car in their driveway when the jack gave way crushing them to death. She watched this event, powerless to assist.

Several weeks later, her other son was killed by a driver running a red light.

We watched her passion for Jesus only intensify. She didn't lie down on the inside but, like David at Ziklag, she "encouraged"[10] herself in the Lord her God. Her worship to Jesus was powerful. Her face shone with a radiance that told us that in her darkest hour it was "well with her soul".[11]

Her powerful, unwavering faith in Jesus inspired and encouraged our congregation. Twenty years later she is still an encouragement to me.

There is a great word in the English language for people who cannot and will not be discouraged. It is "indomitable", which according to Collins Dictionary, it means, "too strong to be defeated or discouraged".[12]

STRONG ENCOURAGERS ARE GIANT KILLERS[13]

A study of the giant of discouragement convinces us that Christians are to be absolute encouragers. We must take every opportunity to encourage our families, our ministry teams, our friends and people we come across all day long.

---

10   1 Samuel 30:6
11   "It is well with my soul." Hymn by Horatio Spafford.
12   Collins Pocket Dictionary p257
13   "Encourage – to inspire with confidence." - Collins Pocket Dictionary, p166.

Have you ever watched crowds of people after church service and noticed a certain person surrounded by a group of smiling people eagerly listening to his words? You can almost guarantee that the person is an encourager, a person instilling self belief and certainty into the lives of those around him. People who are constantly assaulted by the giant of discouragement, struggling under tirades of negativity, are desperately waiting for someone to speak words of courage, which inspires confidence. They long for positive words that build and declare their value.

Every person longs to feel that he is of some value, that he has some significance in a world that constantly endeavours to rob him of any self esteem. Even in the Body of Christ, ministers are usually judged by the size of their churches and placed into categories. Many country pastors never receive a phone call or word of encouragement but labour without money or esteem. Sadly, in the pain of discouragement and loneliness, they often burn out emotionally or fall into an immoral relationship, then face the finger of judgement.

Recently, one of my close friends and ministry colleagues passed away. I had the privilege of conducting his funeral. At his home, large, valuable wreaths of flowers came from ministers across the nation. I heard in conversation:

"It's a pity that in his death all these valuable flowers were sent while in his last few years he couldn't receive a 35-cent phone call."

God is challenging us to confront the giant of discouragement in people's lives with the powerful giant killing weapon of encouragement.

I believe that part of the great success of the ministry of Bishop T.D. Jakes is his marvellous ability to reach down into the lives of hurting people, to inject a powerful awareness of their value to God and significance as greatly loved children of a loving, building, encouraging, Heavenly Father.

SLANDER[14]

One close relative of the giant of discouragement is slander, who is in turn related to the giant false accusation, who is an inbred cousin of the giant jealousy. This evil family of giants do not want you to enjoy success. They also have another family member - laziness. They love to work together strategically to stop your progress.

> *"For I have heard the slander of many: fear was on every side: while they took counsel together against me, they devised to take away my life."* Psalm 31:13

Slander, according to Strong's, is "defaming, evil report and infamy"[15]. In Psalm 31:3, David linked slander with fear and murder.

In Australia, we are privileged to have a church that is a total phenomenon, which is the Hillsong Church in Sydney led by Pastor Brian Houston. This church since its birth some 20 years ago has grown to around 30,000 members and has impacted the world with its brilliant, anointed music. Its conference attracts thousands of people from across the globe, with around 40,000 delegates attending. It is a mighty jewel in the nation's crown. Surely, the nation must draw a sense of pride from its global impact. Surely, the media will exalt and take joy in the amazing success of Hillsong. It seems that the opposite occurs. The previously mentioned family of giants hunt for something that can be splashed across the media. They come with vicious intent to undermine and bring it down. The giant of slander hates success, especially with Christians.

Usually, the greatest key to bringing these giants down is to simply ignore them and then to forcefully put down the accelerator on life and launch out to new heights of achievement. One man said:

> **"Today's newspaper will tomorrow wrap someone's fish and chips or line someone's trash can."**

---

14 "Slander – false and malicious statement about a person." - Collins Pocket Dictionary, p465.
15 Strong's H1681

INTIMIDATION[16]

This enemy seems to be drawn to those who are dreamers and planners - the people of big vision. They come like sharks to the scent of blood in the water when Christians begin to establish their strategies. We only need to look at Joseph in the book of Genesis[17] to know that Satan hates dreamers.

Intimidation is certainly a major giant faced by progressive Christians who wish to move forward.

Intimidation is central in almost every onslaught that giants bring. Goliath is the picture of intimidation. In the field of sport, we can watch opponents constantly using intimidation to gain the advantage.

It is generally agreed by historians that the greatest general in history was Alexander the Great of Macedonia. In the short space of ten years, the young general changed world history.

Alexander was never intimidated by the size of the opposing armies. Often he would face forces five times the size of his own and on certain occasions many times more. My favourite story of Alexander's awesome leadership in the face of massive opposition took place in his foray into India in 326 BC.[18] Here he faced King Porus at the Battle of Hydaspes. Porus certainly became one of Alexander's most respected opponents.

This battle was Alexander's greatest challenge and perhaps his greatest victory. It demanded extraordinary planning and logistics, as some 47,000 troops, 7,500 war horses and all their weapons and equipment of war had to be ferried across a fast moving and treacherous river during a monsoon and into the face of an army greater in strength and skill than any they had ever faced.

In Steven Pressfield's book, Alexander: The Virtues of War, we read a description of the battle in Alexander's own words:

> *"This battle (which was in truth an amphibious assault*
> *in co-ordination with a battle) presented the most*

---

16   "Intimidate – to subdue or influence by fear." - Collins Pocket Dictionary, p265.

17   Genesis 37:19-20

18   Downloaded from: "http://en.wikipedia.org/wiki/Alexander_the_Great#Invasion_of_India"

complex and demanding logistical challenge the army had ever faced – the ferrying, via seven hundred boats and eleven hundred rafts of forty seven thousand men, seventy five hundred horses (the bulk of whom had to be crossed at night and in monsoon), with all their weapons, armour and equipment, including field catapults and stone throwers – and demanded the greatest flexibility and improvisation of widely scattered commanders, many of whom did not speak the same language, across a broad and unprecedented field, against an enemy fighting not for victory alone, but to defend home and liberty. The sheer physical arduousness of the operation beggared all prior endeavours, commencing as it did with an eighteen – mile trek upriver through the mud and thunder of an all night deluge (which indeed hid our movements from the foe but which also turned the channel, already swollen from pre-season downpours into a howling torrent), then mounting to the crossing itself – indeed the swimming, for the last third of a nearly mile-wide river (all this before the battle, even before the marshalling on the far shore, for the battle); then an approach march of fifteen miles, succeeded by a clash across a two mile front, on swampy ground, against 180,000 men, and two hundred war elephants, a force such as no western army had ever seen, let alone confronted and defeated."[19]

Alexander the Great was never intimidated by the size of the enemy, disadvantages of Terrain, weather or obstacles set in his path. He would find a way to turn the things that would halt other generals into the major factor in his continual victories in every battle.

Looking at his position, victory seemed impossible. The following situations would have intimidated most generals of history:

---

19   Alexander: The Virtues of War, p332.

1. He faced an army many times larger than his own and proven in battle.
2. He was on their field of battle.
3. He had to cross a raging river during monsoon season just to enter the battle field.
4. The enemy had, at their front, war elephants by the score that seemed invincible.
5. His cavalry was his trump card always and horses were in dread fear of elephants, thus creating a major change in tactic.
6. His opposition general Porus was a mighty warrior greatly skilled and effective in battle.

Intimidation was something that did not touch Alexander. Alexander never considered that defeat was an option. His mind was set only on victory.
What did he do?

1. His first plan was to do something that his enemy would not expect, which was to cross the river (see the above quote).
2. He turned the strength of Porus' army back on themselves. He used the war elephants for his own advantage. Each elephant had one trainer for life, the Mahood. From a young age, he grew up with the elephant and be its trainer and handler. These men were targeted by the most accurate horseback archers and killed. Control of the beasts was then gone. These incredibly skilled archers and greatly courageous javelin men targeted the eyes and soft underbelly of the elephants, which caused them to turn around in terror and blind rage into their own forces.
3. This opened the way for the operation of the Macedonian lines of Phalanx (long spears) and the forward strength of the infantry.
4. The chaos that this caused, and the discipline and certainty of his men, saw the doors opened for his cavalry to charge into the centre to confront Porus and seize the day.

David was never intimidated. Moses, Joshua and Caleb possessed the attitude that refused to be intimidated.

God wants us to have a transformation in our thought life. We need to develop a mindset that overcomes intimidation by the certainty that God has a strategy and a plan that will turn situations from seeming defeat into total victory.

As Christians, God is constantly reminding us that all we do and achieve for Him hinges on us having a "renewed" and restored mind.[20] One of my favourite scriptures in the Old Testament is Deuteronomy 28:13,

> *"And the LORD shall make thee the head, and not the tail; and thou shalt be above only, and thou shalt not be beneath;..."*

He has made us "more than conquerors".[21] We must establish, through meditation on His Word and strong relationship with Him, a triumphant mindset that cannot be shaken by anything that the giant of intimidation can thrust at us.

FEAR[22]

One giant who constantly roams the arena of faith is fear. This giant is the antithesis of faith. Just as faith produces positive results and brings mighty achievement, fear, timidity and unbelief kept the children of Israel wandering aimlessly for 40 years.

"Courage is not the absence of fear. It is the mastery of it."
Unknown

I have talked with many men who have faced the enemy in the mortal field of combat. My father-in-law was reluctant to discuss World War II with his family, but for some reason, opened up his memories to me. He was a tail gunner in the Lancaster bombers in World War II. He finished two tours of duty decorated with the Distinguished Flying

20   Ephesians 4:23
21   Romans 8:37
22   "Fear – distress or alarm caused by impending danger or pain." - Collins Pocket Dictionary, p183.

Cross and Bar and several mentions in dispatches.

He had flown many times over Germany through the hail of anti-aircraft flak and the blistering onslaught of ME109 fighters that circled in wait for them. Each day, he prepared himself with his Lord knowing, like so many crews of Bomber Command, that this could be his final trip. He had seen so many Lancaster aircraft fall from the sky around him as a blazing fireball, their young crews cut down in the prime of life. Every day he looked death in the eye and, with steely resolve, took his place in the loneliest, most vulnerable and stifling position on the aircraft, as the tail gunner.

Often while flying in the comfort of a jet airliner, I have thought about those young men. Day after day, they crawled into those cold, cramped bombers that rattled and shook their way into the deadly zone. Fragments of hot metal tore into the fuselage of their planes and hopefully avoided vital mechanical components and crew. My father-in-law talked of one crew member who screamed and shrieked for the whole flight back because a large piece of shrapnel had torn his bowel and internal organs to pieces. It was common for ground crews to hose out blood and body parts from the bombers as they hastily patched them up for the next sortie into the killing zone. These men daily looked the giant of death squarely in the eye.

The giant of fear must have constantly whispered into their ears the horrors that lay ahead as they approached the target. Death for these men could come in so many ways. At any moment they could be: torn apart by flying metal, horrendously burned or find themselves in a freefall thousands of feet to their death, parachute out into a hail of metal or find themselves in enemy hands.

Day after day, my father-in-law faced death without reservation. He mastered his fear. When I talked with him, or when I look at his medals displayed on the wall of our home, I think of the inspiring statement:

**"Cowards die a thousand deaths but a brave man
dies but once."**

He must have come to know himself well during that time. The giants he faced so unflinchingly caused me to admire and respect him tremendously. Every day, before he squeezed into the confined spaces of the Lancaster bomber, he had prepared his heart to meet the Christ he loved.

The great champions of Church history confronted giants of a massive scale that sought to crush them but, as they stepped up in victory onto the corpses of these seemingly invincible opponents, they rose in prominence and influence as mighty leaders.

MARTIN LUTHER

When Martin Luther took his famous and historic trip to Worms, he was advised that he would certainly be arrested by Duke George on the road. This was likely to lead to his death as a heretic. His reply roared into the face of the giant of fear:

> **"I tell you if it were to rain Duke George's for nine days, as hard as it could, I would and will go in God's name."**

This is the attitude we must develop when the giant of fear takes the field.

Martin Luther faced the ferocity of Rome and the Papal system. He faced trial and death on every side without flinching. In his own words, Luther describes his attitude to the giants of fear who sought to seize him:

> **"I was born to war with fanatics and devils. Thus my books are very stormy and bellicose. I must root out the stumps and trunks, hew away the thorns and briars, fill in the puddles. I am the rough woodsman who must pioneer and hew a path." Martin Luther**

Those wishing to achieve great Kingdom impact must be prepared to ferociously stand against every satanic obstacle of Hell.

THE APOSTLE PAUL

"For a great door and effectual is opened unto me, and there are many adversaries." 1 Corinthians 16:9

The Apostle Paul must have been confronted by the giant of fear a thousand times. I try to picture in my mind's eye the last days of Paul's life.

I picture a lamp flickering in the dark dampness of the acrid smelling Roman dungeon. Helpless cries, with groans of despair and fear, filled the air. The aged warrior of Christ sat writing his final words that would echo like shafted light into eternity's portals. His lined and chiselled face told endless stories of a giant-conquering hero, who had faced every obstacle and enemy with stoic certainty that in all things he was "more than a conqueror"[23].

I picture Paul pull his robe over his scarred shoulders. His body bore the statement of a man of God who had defiantly faced the giant of fear again and again. I see him gaze into the darkness of his cell. His eyes burn with exhilaration and certain fire that no opponent or circumstance he had faced could extinguish. With unshakeable certainty, he wrote:

"For I am now ready to be offered, and the time of my departure is at hand." 2 Timothy 4:6

His lips must have curled with the satisfied sense of victory, as he wrote:

"I have fought a good fight, I have finished my course, I have kept the faith". 2 Timothy 4:7

---

23   Romans 8:37

Only God knew what horrors Nero would devise for his death but it mattered little. The giant of fear had long since been expelled. Intimidation and anxiety were totally swallowed up by the awesome, pulsing majesty within and the utter thrill of extraordinary conquests faced and won, as the gospel of the Kingdom with mighty signs had changed the world forever.

Behind him lay massive churches, full of God's power, cities shaken to the foundations, cultures challenged and found wanting, indeed a world that would never be the same again.

The great gladiator and general of God had seized the Kingdom of God with the most "ardent zeal" and "intense exertion"[24] Giants that had opposed him on every side had fallen like Dagon before the Ark of God.[25] Paul was a giant killer, a warrior of strength and unstoppable zeal and exertion. He had stepped up onto carcass after carcass of giants that had been slain about him, by his anointed hand. Death presented no fear. In fact, it seems he welcomed it as a friend. The method mattered not at all. He had carried within himself the sentence of death for years. No giant had any impact or influence over God's man.

The giants of intimidation and fear love to make their presence strongly felt on the front line of evangelism.

As I write these words, I sit in my hotel room and prepare for a major open air meeting in the city of Lahore, Pakistan. Last night, the glory of God flooded the stadium. Crippled children walked, tumours vanished, deaf ears opened and broken bones were restored. Today, I am aware of the seriousness of our position. This is the front line and the giant of intimidation is taunting my mind.

It is most interesting that on the walls of my hotel room are two Mogul prints of public beheadings. I think God has a great sense of humour. I feel a strange mixture of the awesomeness of God and a deep sense of apprehension. There is a real awareness that last night's release of power has brought us out from under the radar in a hostile environment. It is amazing how a tirade of taunts and threats begin to assault my mind. Giants begin to stand in my face, yet the mighty

24   Matthew 11:12 Amplified Bible
25   1 Samuel 5:4

Holy Ghost arises up like a torrent of fire in my belly and supernatural resolve fills my inner man with steely strength.

Are we giants or grasshoppers?

We are the unstoppable, mighty, Holy Ghost-charged, giant killers of God. Tonight, we step into the great arena of faith, clothed with the full armour of God, as unstoppable gladiators in this great global conquest.

GIANT KILLERS LOOK DEATH IN THE EYE AND LAUGH

In the movie '300', a Persian envoy, in an attempt to intimidate and bring fear to the 300 Spartans at Thermopylae, tells them that the sky will be made black with their arrows. The Spartan warrior, with a grin of defiance, declares, "Then we will fight them in the shade".

DEBT

One of the most lethal enemies we can face is the giant of debt. This giant gains legal control of our lives, often by our own decisions. This giant can cause our dreams and purposes of life to come to a grinding halt.

Many Christians, instead of impacting the Kingdom of God, spend their time weighed down, disillusioned and paralysed by the overshadowing giant of debt. This giant is constantly there, declaring his control and ownership. This giant is one of the most vicious enemies that we can face. God is calling on us to smash the power of debt, look this giant in the eye and purposefully confront and totally subdue it. This giant may be produced through: bad financial choices, lack of discipline, poor planning, stepping out in presumption, trying to "keep up with the Joneses" by living beyond our means, betrayals, as a result of sickness, poor management or direct satanic opposition. I once heard the powerful South African preacher, Dr Rodney Howard Browne declare:

"I'm an anointed sheriff driving that poverty devil out of town."

Whatever its cause, this giant is a great intimidator. It speaks constantly and casts its shadow over all of our endeavours.

GIANTS HAVE WEAPONS

When Goliath confronted Saul's army he certainly carried frightening weapons: a massive sword and spear. His major weapons, however, were psychological: intimidation, fear, slander and discouragement.

EXAMPLE OF WEAPONS

When David came to the field of battle the first weapon that confronted him was in the mouth of his own brother Eliab.

Eliab assaulted young David with a tirade of slanderous, discouraging words that were sent forth to shut down what cowardly Eliab saw only as a youthful, pride-filled zeal in his young brother.

EFFECTIVENESS OF THE WEAPONS

No giant in scripture, no matter how intimidating or ferocious, was ever successful against God's people.

Did they intimidate? Absolutely!

Did they taunt? Ferociously!

Did their words echo defiantly with supernatural seemingly invincible force? Always!

Did they ever succeed in killing a mighty man or woman of God? On no occasion!

Were their weapons of battle ever used against a child of God? No! No! No! They were only turned against themselves by the hand of God's gladiators.

A study of all the giants in scripture reveals that, despite their armour, their massive size, and their formidable weaponry, not one giant at any stage defeated or even, it seems, wounded a man or woman of God. They boasted, intimidated, opposed, harassed and mentally bombarded. At times, they immobilised or paralysed simply by their words and ferocity but they never struck a fatal blow – not one.

In fact, the only weapons of any giant that proved successful were actually used against themselves. Benaiah snatched the spear (the size of a weaver's beam) out of the hands of the giant and drove it back through his body. Goliath intimidated and terrified an army but it was his own sword, in the hands of a teenage freckle-faced youth, that severed his giant head.

It seems that the very weapon that the giants use to taunt us can be seized by us and mightily driven back to destroy them that taunt us.

> *"No weapon that is formed against thee shall prosper; and every tongue that shall rise against thee in judgment thou shalt condemn. This is the heritage of the servants of the LORD, and their righteousness is of me, saith the LORD."* Isaiah 54:17

GOD'S GIANT KILLERS

A study of the Scriptures reveals a unique group of warriors who not only defeated giants individually but were responsible for the final eradication of all the giants on the earth. They were the "eradicators" of giants.

The following is the list of those mighty men who were not fazed, held back or overcome by these huge terrifying enemies but have engraved their names on God's honour role.

It would be good to study the exploits of each warrior for yourself.

- Moses killed Og of Bashan, a massive giant king whose iron bed was approximately 4.3 m (14 feet) long and 1.8 m (6 feet) wide (Deuteronomy 3:11).

- Caleb, in his late 80s, killed Arba the brutal ruling Anakim of Kirjath-Arba (later Hebron), along with the giant rulers Sheshai, Ahiman and Talmai (Joshua 14:15).
- General Joshua and his forces utterly slaughtered all the Anakim giants from Hebron, Debir, Anab and all the mountains of Judah and Israel, which left only a remnant in Gaza, Gath and Ashdod (Joshua 11:21-22).
- The shepherd boy David destroyed Goliath of Gath, the Philistine champion (1 Samuel 17).
- David's mighty men were God's instruments that killed the remaining giants.
- Abishai killed Ishbibenob (2 Samuel 21:17).
- Sibbechai the Hushathite killed Saph (2 Samuel 21:18).
- Elhanan the son of Jaareoregim from Bethlehem killed Lahmi the brother of Goliath of Gath (2 Samuel 21:19).
- Jonathan the son of Shimea, David's brother, killed the great giant with six fingers on each hand and six toes on each foot (2 Samuel 21:20).
- Benaiah drove the giant's own spear back through his body to slay a 2.75 m (9 foot) tall giant of Egypt and (1 Chronicles 11:22-23).

After these men completed their assignments, no giants were found on the earth.

This book is not directed to Christians who will just stand against the giant obstacles spawned in Hell to confront them, but those who, by the sword of the Spirit, the power of the Holy Ghost and raw courage, will be "eradicators", ruthless warriors of God called to mighty exploits in the day of God's power.

In the coming chapters, we will study God's giant killers examining their unique characters, passions and methods. I trust that they will inspire you as much as they have thrilled and challenged me.

2
MOSES

"IF GOD BE FOR US, WHO CAN BE AGAINST US?"

The first recorded giant killer we read of in Scripture may come as a surprise. It was Moses. Moses was not just Israel's delivering leader. He was a warrior of renown. It is also significant that he was over 100-years-old when he killed Og of Bashan.

As Moses had faced giants of many forms, the giant Og of Bashan, whose bed measured 4.1 m (13½ feet) by 1.8 m (6 feet), was little challenge to this Kingdom gladiator.

ENCOUNTERS WITH GOD FORGE GIANT KILLERS

Moses must have shaken with terror decades before as he gazed at a sight that no man had ever seen. The peak of the rugged Sinai Mountains blazed with the swirling supernatural presence of the God, the great "I AM", who had declared himself as a "devouring fire"[1]. Lightning flashed as the great God who had opened the Red Sea with "the blast of the breath of His nostrils"[2] summoned His man into His own terrifying presence. The great cry of God's heart has never changed: He still woos and calls His giant killers to draw close, to leave the hustle and bustle of everyday life and to come into His fiery, all-consuming presence. Here, He shapes "new sharp threshing instruments" that will "thresh the mountains".

---

1   Exodus 24:17
2   2 Samuel 22:16

"Behold, I will make thee a new sharp threshing instrument having teeth: thou shalt thresh the mountains, and beat them small, and shalt make the hills as chaff." Isaiah 41:15

This was a far cry from the first encounter at the burning bush or even the awesome demonstration of judgment that Moses saw poured out on Egypt. Moses describes for us the scene that confronted him:

"And Mount Sinai was altogether on a smoke, because the Lord descended upon it in fire: and the smoke thereof ascended as the smoke of a furnace, and the whole mount quaked greatly." Exodus 19:18

"And all the people saw the thunderings, and the lightnings and the noise of the trumpet, and the mountain smoking: and when the people saw it, they removed, and stood afar off." Exodus 20:18

"And so terrible was the sight, that Moses said, 'I exceedingly fear and quake'" Hebrews 12:21

A boundary was placed about the foot of Mount Sinai and the death penalty was put in place for anyone, even an animal, that crossed it.

Moses was summoned by God's audible voice, crossed the boundary and came up into the fiery spectacle from which the people fled.

"...and the Lord called Moses up to the top of the mount; and Moses went up." Exodus 19:20b

For 40 days, Moses stayed in the undiluted splendour and glory of God in preparation for the awesome, eternal task for which he had been appointed.

No giant Moses ever faced was as terrifying and daunting as this lonely climb up the rocky outcrops of Sinai into the majestic inexplicable glory of God. Compared with this experience, giants, no matter how large, would have looked like mere insects to Moses. Terror must have seized him as he looked up into the fury that lit up the mountain peaks around him. Sinai was supernaturally ablaze, a terrifying glorious spectacle of the presence of God Himself. After going up into this, no army that he ever faced, no giant that he confronted could terrify or intimidate him. He had lived in the splendour of God's glory. He neither ate nor drank during that time as God pulsed and coursed through every cell and fibre of his being. Who or what could stand against him now? He had witnessed God's awesome acts that had seen the might of Egypt swallowed up in the Red Sea. He had seen God's fearsome wrath unleashed on Egypt, in a way never seen before and now he had actually dwelt in God's undiluted glory.

God had indelibly burnt into Moses' psyche, the certainty of God's total purpose and commitment. No doubt was left in his heart that God had called him, anointed him and gone before him with miraculous might. Moses recites to us the word of certainty that God had spoken to him regarding his future campaigns:

> *"For my Angel shall go before thee, and bring thee in unto the Amorites and the Hittites and the Perizzites and the Canaanites, the Hivites, and the Jebusites: and I will cut them off."* Exodus 23:23

> *"And I will send my fear before thee, and will destroy all the people to whom thou shalt come, and I will make all thine enemies turn their backs unto thee."* Exodus 23:27

> *"By little and little I will drive them out from before thee, until thou be increased and inherit the land."* Exodus 23:30

Moses knew God intimately and He knew His word. God's promises now invaded his every thought. He knew that with God nothing could stop him, only the unbelief and rebellion of a stiff-necked nation.

When we taste the reality of Heaven and choose to live our lives in the throne room of His power, what can Satan possibly use to intimidate us or stop our progress?

It is the awesome encounters with God, these times so intimate where Heaven invades our heart, that take us with bold resolve to confront all that Hell can throw against us.

Moses had experienced the inexplicable power and intimate presence of God on Sinai, so no direct attack on him could succeed. The real giant Moses would face would not be a mere Og of Bashan and his army but the soul-destroying unbelief and faithlessness of his own people.

MOSES FACED THE GIANT OF TOTAL FRUSTRATION

It was God who instructed Moses to send the twelve spies into the Promised Land. Grief and devastation must have gripped this fearless warrior of God when they returned, defeated and afraid, with a report that the Promised Land could not be taken. What must Moses have felt among this "stiff-necked", cowardly people? No doubt the giant of overwhelming frustration must have shouted in his face every day of the 40 long and arduous years as they aimlessly wandered the Sinai Peninsula. Imagine wandering for 40 years with an unbelieving, cowardly crowd of millions. This would be the worst giant that Moses ever faced. Those 40 years of wandering with this frustration must have driven him to a point of distraction. As he watched and shared the unquenchable faith and desire of Joshua and Caleb, as they spoke and discussed the Promised Land, it possibly kept him purposely moving forward. He must have hungered and craved for the days when the cloud came down over the Tabernacle and he was summoned into the presence of God to commune with Him as friend.

How many anointed men and women have lost heart and walked

away from the call and purpose of God because they were surrounded by churches full of unbelieving Christians who were totally resistant to change and fresh challenges? How often have men of God been stifled from godly impact by deacon boards who resisted opportunities to step out into large endeavours or, through fear, failed to back new and revolutionary God-inspired ventures?

The frustration that Moses felt among the people had to be faced daily, as the nations opposed them and confronted them en-route to Jordan and they were savagely dealt with. Under Moses' leadership, these nations were ferociously crushed and their cities and towns seized but the frustration of this unbelieving generation was his constant "thorn in the flesh".[3] The pitiful complaining and murmuring ultimately drove Moses to strike the rock in anger.

The Scripture tells us that the people "chided with Moses"[4], groaning and despairing until Moses reacted in anger. The word translated as "chide" means, "to grapple, hold a controversy, complain and contend".[5]

Matthew Henry's commentary says:

> **"They spoke the same absurd and brutish language that their fathers had done before them. They wished they had died as malefactors by the hands of divine justice, rather than thus seem for a while neglected by the divine mercy."**

Moses gives us one of the greatest lessons in dealing with this giant onslaught. He, with Aaron, walked away from the flesh, with all of its complaints, and threw themselves down on their faces before the Lord.[6]

"And the glory of the LORD appeared unto them."

---

3   2 Corinthians 12:7
4   Numbers 20:3
5   Strong's H7378
6   Numbers 20:6

He instructed Moses to speak to the rock. God did not judge but wanted to humble them by His gracious provision.

Moses should have taken check of his response. The complaining, murmuring, judging giant had worn him down to a place where, while he carried the mighty anointing of God, harshness and fleshly weakness oozed out of him as he addressed the people. You can hear the sharp, sarcastic bite of his words and sense his frustration as the rod smashed twice into the rock.

This action cost him entrance into the Promised Land. How often have people of God reacted so sharply to the giant of frustration that they have lashed out verbally or physically and it costs them incredibly?

Moses shows us exactly how to react at first. Walk from the situation and throw ourselves down before the One who can step in. We should not leave that place with the anger still burning but recognise where the onslaught is coming from, who the giant really is and vent our feelings with words of authority in the spirit realm and spend some time in the strong praise of God.

It was this giant of frustration that confronted Moses day after day, the murmuring and pitiful complaining, that ultimately drove Moses to strike the rock in anger.

The giant of frustration should cause us to rise up with more savage and calculated resolve, with Kingdom authority, not with fleshly expression. Frustration will often be the catalyst that causes us to step out and attempt the impossible. Moses in all other situations certainly proved a mighty slayer of giants.

The route to Jordan was constantly opposed, foolishly and unjustly. Whatever opponents stood against Moses were ruthlessly smashed and great possessions taken. When Sihon King of Heshbon opposed him he was crushed and his many cities seized.

Moses had dwelt in the awesome presence of God. He knew God intimately in a way that no other knew Him. The certainty of who he was and who had gone before him, fuelled by the utter frustration of an unbelieving generation made him a formidable unstoppable opponent who could not be defeated. Moses' life gives us an insight into a ferocious, calculated and complete decimation of his enemies. Only the pitiful murmurings of his people could ultimately stop him.

*"Then Sihon came out against us, he and all his people,
to fight at Jahaz.
And the Lord our God delivered him before us; and we
smote him, and his sons, and all his people.
And we took all his cities at that time, and utterly
destroyed the men, and the women, and the little ones,
of every city, we left none to remain: ..."*
Deuteronomy 2:32-34

Og of Bashan was truly a giant of giants. He was the largest giant
mentioned who confronted the people of God. His iron bedstead was
4.1 m (13 feet) long and 1.8 m (6 feet) wide. He was a massive man, at
least 3.65 m (12 feet) tall. His massive cities were:

" *...fenced with high walls, gates, and bars; beside
unwalled towns a great many." Deuteronomy 3:5b*

After his mighty encounters with God, Og of Bashan, despite his
enormous size and fury, must have seemed to Moses like a grasshopper
to be crushed. This would have been the case with every opponent
that Moses faced.

Moses and Israel crushed and totally annihilated this army and race.
In all, they took possession of 60 cities, many unwalled towns and
great tracts of land.

Moses seemed to wade through all opposition like a hot knife
through butter. His extraordinary, supernatural encounters with God
on Sinai's mountain peaks assured that any battle in the valleys or
plains would be speedily won.

Our challenge as giant killers is to take the time to climb the rugged
outcrops of our mountain of encounter and boldly enter and dwell
in the fiery, throne room presence of God's glory. The more time
we spend in the awesomeness of God's glory, the smaller and less
significant the giants we confront will seem.

MOSES
DEMONSTRATOR OF GOD'S POWER

"And there arose not a prophet since in Israel like unto Moses, whom the LORD knew face to face, In all the signs and the wonders, which the LORD sent him to do in the land of Egypt to Pharaoh, and to all his servants, and to all his land, And in all that mighty hand, and in all the great terror which Moses shewed in the sight of all Israel." Deuteronomy 34:10-12

Moses was a demonstrator of mighty signs and wonders. This awesome loading of God's power that flowed so ferociously from him, grew out of this statement: "whom the Lord knew face to face". Here is the great key to the demonstration of the power that crushed a giant, scattered Pharaoh and delivered a nation.

Moses didn't know God from a distance. He knew him "face to face". The word "knew" in the Hebrew is "yada"[7] which speaks of intimate knowledge – the intimate knowledge of husband and wife.

We see from the following scripture that those who do know their God achieve outstanding results.

"And such as do wickedly against the covenant shall he corrupt by flatteries: but the people that do know their God shall be strong, and do exploits."
Daniel 11:32

- Moses didn't know about God – he knew Him personally and intimately.
- Moses didn't just know His ways – he knew experientially the undiluted splendour of His glory.
- Moses didn't just declare good messages – he walked out of the Throne Room physically illuminated with the tangible substance of God's glory.

---

7   Strong's H3045

- Moses didn't come up with good strategies and plans from board room and committee meetings – he walked out of the fiery, terrifying glory and splendour of God, with the exact pattern of God's purpose.

The great men and women of God in Scripture and in history walked out of the presence of God, alive with His power and certain of the purpose of God.

Elijah walked, supernaturally charged, out of the lonely, windswept region of Tishbe in Gilead, after he had desperately sought "the face" of God, into the throne room of King Ahab with the very elements of nature at the command of his words.

We talk of "seeking the face" of God. Do we fully understand what it means? We are seeking that place with God, the Throne Room, where the "lightnings" of God flash and the "thunderings" roar. We seek to gaze upon the splendour of Him "who sits on the throne" blazing with divine fire and blinding light. We are seeking the Father's heart of love so intimately boundless that we will be drawn into and swallowed up by its eternal billows. We are seeking to press into that realm of unspeakable awe that causes even the six winged Seraphim to shield their eyes and cover their feet because of His infinite splendour.

This place is more than a Bible training college or the place where we can find six keys to successful living. This is the place where we are engulfed with God. This is where we learn to harness the unlimited dimension of the power of God that already fills us. It is the place where we move from a "nice" walk with God to the demonstration of signs, wonders and the miracles that will shake the nations.

THIS GOSPEL IS A DEMONSTRATED GOSPEL

When Paul wrote to the Corinthian church, he reminded them of his approach:

> *"And my speech and my preaching was not with enticing words of man's wisdom, but in demonstration of the Spirit and of power"* 1 Corinthians 2:4

He explained to them that he did not want their faith to stand on men's wisdom "but on the power of God".[8]

Jesus was so clear regarding the need for the Kingdom to be demonstrated that He said:

> *"If I do not the works of my Father, believe me not. But if I do, though ye believe not me, believe the works: that ye may know, and believe, that the Father [is] in me, and I in him."* John 10:37-38

The baptism in the Holy Spirit is more than just a wonderful experience. It is an "arming for war". It is the launching pad to the demonstration of the power of God.

As I've travelled the world, preaching the gospel for over 30 years, my passion has always been to see the mighty demonstration of the power of God. Jesus said:

> *"...this gospel of the kingdom shall be preached in all the world for a witness unto all nations; and then shall the end come."* Matthew 24:14

Notice He said "this gospel of the kingdom" shall be preached - this same gospel that He preached with the same mighty signs and wonders. In fact He said we would do "greater works"[9].

---

8   1 Corinthians 2:5
9   John 14:12

This gospel is a demonstrated gospel. Praise God that all over the world there is a fresh hunger to see the mighty works of God demonstrated.

We read in Acts that Jesus was "approved of God...by miracles and wonders and signs"[10], and that He "went about doing good, and healing all that were oppressed of the devil; for God was with him."[11]

We read in Romans that Paul powerfully preached and demonstrated Christ to the Gentiles making them:

> "...obedient, by word and deed, Through mighty signs and wonders, by the power of the Spirit of God; so that from Jerusalem, and round about unto Illyricum, I have fully preached the gospel of Christ." Romans 15:18-19

Moses was a demonstrator of God's power. Scripture tells us that he operated:

> "In all the signs (Hebrew oth[12] - miraculous proofs) and the wonders, (Hebrew mopheth[13] - wonderful, authenticating deeds, mighty acts of God) which the Lord sent him to do in the land of Egypt to Pharaoh, and to all his servants, and to all his land (signs and wonders to shake an entire nation) And in all that mighty hand (Hebrew yad[14] - power, strength and mighty outstretched arm) and in all the great terror (stupendous, wonderful, terrible, deeds) which Moses showed in the sight of all Israel." Deuteronomy 34:11-12 (additions mine)

---

10   Acts 2:22
11   Acts 10:38
12   Strong's H226
13   Strong's H4159
14   Strong's H3027

Moses showed forth the awesome signs, wonders, undeniable, authenticating acts and terrifying, stupendous, wonderful mighty deeds of his God whom he knew "face to face" in unique intimacy. Surely these same characteristics should follow God anointed giant killers of today.

No wonder the giants before Moses were like grasshoppers or cockroaches to be crushed.

For years now I have studied the lives of God's great warriors. In our own lifetime we have seen men and women of God rise up to demonstrate and show forth God's mighty outstretched hand and see whole nations shaken to their foundations.

In the 1950s, Tommy Hicks was an evangelist travelling around the USA. Within him was a great hunger for God and a desire to significantly demonstrate the power of God.

Recently, after telling Tommy's story in one of my sermons, I sat with a man who had travelled with him and studied under him. He told me I had accurately related his story.

Tommy was dissatisfied in his walk and impact for God. He began to press in to God in prayer. While ministering in a certain town in the USA he had a dream. God showed him a massive wheat field in the shape of South America and placed in his hand a sickle for harvesting. He became aware that he was about to embark on a continent shaking campaign. Back at the church where he was ministering, he was greeted by the pastor's wife who told him that she had seen him in a dream going into the great wheat field of South America with a large reaping sickle.

Tommy knew that he had heard from God and that he was moving into a great date with destiny.

Tommy took on board God's plan and set himself to fast and pray. He fasted for 40 days "seeking God's face". He didn't feel as though he had really come into that place with God so he fasted again for 40 days. Again, he still felt he wanted to press in more so when physically able, he fasted a third 40-day fast.[15]

At the end of this fast God met him profoundly. Significant encounters with God often come during long periods of fasting and prayer.

15   It is very unwise to unadvisedly launch into long periods of fasting.

God instructed Tommy to cancel all ministry in the USA and fly to South America. As he flew to Argentina a short time later with a clear mandate from the Lord, God spoke to him, "Go and talk to Mr Peron" . "Who is Mr Peron?" he wondered, so he asked the airline stewardess who this man Peron would be.

"That, sir," she replied, "is our President."

Therefore, his first mission was to go to the President and explain his purpose in coming to Argentina. Government officials were less than helpful in this matter and politely explained how near to impossible it would be for him to speak with the President.

While they debated the subject, a man crippled in his legs from polio limped into the room.

"Bring that man to me," said Tommy.

A sudden demonstration of power in Jesus' name saw crippled limbs straighten and strengthen to normality. Within a very short space of time, a meeting with a most interested Mr Peron was arranged. He questioned Tommy Hicks regarding his purpose in coming to Argentina. Tommy boldly declared his mandate for the people of Argentina to be saved and miraculously healed by the power of God. Mr Peron then explained to Tommy the terrible skin condition that he suffered from and asked if he could be healed.

Again, in Jesus' name, Tommy demonstrated the power of God and the condition vanished from the President's body.

President Peron then called the leading newspaper men to a press conference. He urged them to write whatever Tommy wanted to say and do. He arranged for the radio stations and the giant football stadiums to be made available to him for his purpose.

Within days, he preached to the largest crowds, to that time, seen in the history of the Christian church. Numbers were recorded at over 400,000 in meetings. The demonstration of power was so great that trucks and tractor trailers had to be driven onto the grounds to be loaded with the sticks, crutches and wheelchairs that had been discarded all over the fields. A whole nation, in days, had been swept by the mighty, demonstrated power of God.

During the great healing and miracle crusades of the 1950s, people like F.F. Bosworth, A.A. Allen, William Branham and many great evangelists operated in mighty signs and wonders to such a degree that fleets of trucks were called in to carry away sticks, crutches and discarded wheelchairs from their great crusade meetings.

It has been estimated, that in 50 days of ministry in Argentina, close to one million souls came into the Kingdom under Hicks' ministry.

This is indeed a time where all the global circumstances point to a fresh, unprecedented wave of conviction and miracle power.

Bookshops across the Western world have whole sections dedicated to the occult, the new age, witchcraft and psychic healers. The massive increase in the sales of these books bears witness to a huge spiritual hunger in the hearts of vast multitudes of people. How devastating that so many ministers today are endeavouring to build their churches on worldly methods leaving the "new-agers" to woo the multitudes whose heart is crying out for spiritual things.

Some years ago, I preached at the famous "Melodyland" church in Anaheim, California where Kathryn Kuhlman had often preached. I was reminded that, in one of her great healing crusade meetings held in Los Angeles, it was recorded that 63 people stepped out of wheelchairs in one meeting.

We have a God-given mandate, like Tommy Hicks, to carry and demonstrate God's miracle power to a desperate world.

Recently, while ministering at a miracle crusade in Papua New Guinea, we saw an exceptional flow of power. The miracles we witnessed were thrilling but one was simply breathtaking.

A man had been carried on a stretcher into the meeting. Cancer, which commenced in his feet, had spread through his body and he was bedridden, in fact, paralysed, for the previous six months. He appeared ashen grey and obviously near death.

After I preached the Word, I challenged the sick to act on their faith and begin to do what had been impossible previously. Things began to happen across the crowd. As I looked to my right side, I noticed a group of men who stood and kneeled beside the paralysed man. His arms and legs began to move. Slowly they helped him to his feet. I watched him take small uncertain steps. These became progressively stronger, as the previously dead limbs began to free up. As we looked, it became apparent that on the soles of his feet were huge growths making him at least 7.6 cm (3 inches) taller. Suddenly, before our eyes, these growths vanished and he stood flat on the floor. He walked strongly.

Amazingly, the following night he came by taxi to the National Stadium and sat in pouring rain and listened to the word of God. I shared the story of the man's healing to a most responsive but wet crowd. One of our team excitedly said, "He's here!" We watched him beam with utter exhilaration as he came up onto the platform. His face shone and he looked as fit as an Olympic athlete. What a mighty God we serve! He is the great Demonstrator.

Like Moses of old we have been called to preach and demonstrate the power of God. In Acts 4:33 we read that:

> "...with great power gave the apostles witness of the
> resurrection of the Lord Jesus: and great grace was
> upon them all."

With great demonstration of the power of God, we are called to show the world that Jesus is truly raised from the dead.

MOSES MENTORED THE NEXT GENERATION

Moses saw in Joshua a tremendous hunger for God and knew that he was to invest his whole life into this young man. His desire was not just to teach and instruct him but to impart the anointing of God into his life and shape and mould him into a conquering, giant killing general like himself.

> *"And Joshua the son of Nun was full of the spirit of wisdom; for Moses had laid his hands upon him: and the children of Israel hearkened unto him, and did as the LORD commanded Moses."* Deuteronomy 34:9

Moses not only mentored, charged and continually exhorted Joshua but imparted to him of the spirit that was so powerfully operating in through and on him.

> *"And the LORD said unto Moses, Take thee Joshua the son of Nun, a man in whom is the spirit, and lay thine hand upon him.*
> *And set him before Eleazar the priest, and before all the congregation; and give him a charge in their sight.*
> *And thou shalt put some of thine honour upon him, that all the congregation of the children of Israel may be obedient."* Numbers 27:18-20

We must be preparing the next generation. The giant killers in scripture raised giant killers to follow them. Our success in ministry will be judged by the strength and impact of the next generation of disciples that we mentor and release.

Moses mentored his famous mighty men, Joshua and Caleb and a whole generation of conquerors, Joshua became a mighty general and mentor, Caleb mentored Othniel the first Judge while David mentored and raised up a group of mighty men of renown and valour.

Who are we raising up under us? The success we have in our generation must be magnified to much greater heights in the coming generation.

MOSES - AGED WARRIOR

Age has never entered God's equation in the area of faith. Moses didn't even start his great commission till he was 80-years-old. Sarah, with a huge grin on her face, pushed a pram at over 90-years-old. The pram was filled with a bouncing baby boy that was born to herself and her husband Abraham who was almost 100-years-old. Both Joshua and Caleb were conquering generals in their 80s. Age must never cause us to stop dreaming and planning. We have the certain promise that in the last days, "...old men shall dream dreams"[16].

Moses at 120-years-old was dynamically fit and vibrant right to his death.

> *"And Moses was a hundred and twenty years old when he died: his eye was not dim (weak, dull faint or failing)[17] nor his natural force (freshness, vigor, manly strength)[18] abated."* Deuteronomy 34:7 (additions mine)

Caleb (as we will see in the coming chapters) at 85-years-old was a honed, fit, dynamic warrior.

In recent times some of Christianty's greatest heroes have done their most significant exploits after they reached 60-years-old.

Smith Wigglesworth, the great healing apostle (1859-1947) was 48-years-old when he (an illiterate plumber) was powerfully baptised with the Holy Spirit.

The greatest impact of this man of God occurred from 60-years-old on to his death at the age of 88.

Reinhard Bonnke, possibly the greatest soul winner in history, has seen more souls saved to Christ since reaching 60-years-old than in all his previous ministry combined.

Age must not ever be a consideration of a giant killer.

16   Acts 2:17
17   Strong's H3543
18   Strong's H3893

"Aging is not 'lost youth' but a new stage of
opportunity and strength."
Betty Friedan 1921-2006

"It is a mistake to regard age as a downhill grade
toward dissolution. The reverse. As one grows older,
one climbs with surprising strides."
George Sand (1804-1876)[19]

CONCLUSION

Moses the giant killer had three main characteristics that have
impacted my life.

1.   He knew God intimately. He learned to abide and live in the
undiluted splendour of God's awesome presence.
2.   He was a mighty warrior of God, and impacted nations with
incredible, miraculous demonstration.
3.   He was mentor to a whole giant killing generation.

KEYS FROM MOSES THE GIANT KILLER

Whenever we read of giants in scripture there are certain consistencies:

- They oppose and defy.
- They aim to resist and stop progress.
- They refuse entry.

On the opposite side of the coin, destruction of them has certain consistent results:

- Freedom of forward movement is assured.
- Possession of goods, land and influence always accompany victory over them.
- Greater fear and dread rises in other enemies.
- Stature, strength and influence rise to new levels in our lives.

1. Moses had been on the mountain top with God. He was not a man of theory but a man who had learned to live in the awareness of God's unlimited power and intimacy with His ways. Here is our challenge. People who intimately know their God will never be halted by the intimidation of giants. "They are the breakfast of champions."[20] Og the giant in comparison with the terrifying splendour and resistless power of God must have seemed like a fly to be swatted.

   "But the people that do know their God shall be strong and do exploits." Daniel 11:32b

2. Moses knew the promises of God and the certainty of God's faithfulness and covenant. The clarity of these promises was clear to Moses as we read in Scripture that he quoted them and declared them continually, especially to Joshua.

"...there hath not failed one word of all his good promise, which he promised by the hand of Moses his servant." 1 Kings 8:56b

He knew the land God had promised His people, he knew the power of God and constantly declared his "possession".

3. Moses makes it very clear that as Israel moved out in conquest that God would go before them and fight for them.

"Then I said unto you, Dread not, neither be afraid of them.
The Lord your God which goeth before you, he shall fight for you, according to all that he did for you in Egypt before your eyes." Deuteronomy 1:29-30

Every time I have stepped out, having firstly gained God's certainty in my heart that He has gone ahead, I have seen the most extraordinary outpourings of God's power.

JOSHUA

ERADICATOR OF GIANTS

"And at that time came Joshua, and cut off the Anakims from the mountains, from Hebron, from Debir, from Anab, and from all the mountains of Judah, and from all the mountains of Israel: Joshua destroyed them utterly with their cities. There was none of the Anakims left in the land of the children of Israel: only in Gaza, in Gath, and in Ashdod, there remained (remnants)."
Joshua 11: 21-22

Joshua is the awesome general of conquest. He is not a mere giant killer, but a giant eradicator. He didn't just expel the giants he faced. He systematically utterly destroyed them and their cities, "…from Hebron, from Debir, from Anab, and from all the mountains of Judah, and from all the mountains of Israel". Joshua led his men like a giant threshing machine.

God spoke to Reinhard Bonnke some years ago saying:

> **"I am taking the sickle out of your hand and giving you a combine harvester."**

Joshua was born to a family of slaves. He was part of the miraculous deliverance from Egypt and saw the strength of God's mighty arm. He became Moses' servant from a youth[1] and served a long, but thorough, apprenticeship under him to learn the ways of God, leadership in <u>battle and absolut</u>e dependence on the word of God. He is the picture

---

1   Numbers 11:28

of a loyal servant, a strong decisive leader, a man of total integrity and a man totally committed to God and His word.

A study of this awesome giant killer reveals a single-minded warrior of extraordinary character and single-minded purpose. In battle and conquest for the Promised Land he was thorough in preparation as he sent spies in to accurately assess all possibilities and outcomes. He planned the conquests prayerfully, with his ears tuned to every detail that God spelled out for him. After he assessed every detail and planned thoroughly, Joshua went against the enemies with ruthless, surgical thoroughness. He never compromised but sought to fulfil every command of the Lord with military precision.

Like Caleb, Joshua was an old man in this great conquest, an old ruthless man who caused the enemies of God to tremble with fear and terror. It is amazing when we consider that like Caleb this old general of God was over 85-years-old.

What then are the characteristics we need to glean from General Joshua?

1. JOSHUA WAS HUNGRY FOR GOD'S ANOINTING

"And the LORD spake unto Moses face to face, as a man speaketh unto his friend. And he turned again into the camp: but his servant Joshua, the son of Nun, a young man, departed not out of the tabernacle." Exodus 33:11

Joshua must have longed for the encounters with God experienced by his great mentor Moses. Moses was so utterly dependent on God that unless the glory and presence of God went with him, he did not wish to move ahead. Joshua must have heard Moses pray like this:

"...If thy presence go not with me, carry us not up hence."[2]

Young Joshua had seen the glory on Mount Sinai, albeit from a distance. He had seen the cloud descend upon the tabernacle so many times and had watched Moses go in and return with his face so illuminated by the glory of God that he had to wear a veil to hide the splendour.

2　　Exodus 33:15a

How the apprentice must have envied the privileged place that Moses enjoyed with his God. He must have talked often with Moses of the great Sinai encounters and asked numerous questions about the personal talks Moses shared with his Friend.

"As I was with Moses so I shall be with you."[3]

Moses had set the example of intimacy with God clearly and precisely as the vital key to leadership. Joshua grew in the knowledge that a leader in the great exploits of God must be a person who intimately knows the person of his God and the awesome, tangible power of His presence. He learned from Moses that great exploits are birthed from the Throne Room of God.

When Moses went into the holiest place of the Tabernacle, he spoke to God face-to-face as a friend, then emerged with his face alight with the radiance of God's glory. The people waited in awe to see the glory on Moses, just to glimpse the fleeting afterglow of the God encounter. Joshua, however, stayed back as close as the law permitted to the Holy Place, just to catch and absorb whatever remained of the mighty cloud of glory that hung as an afterglow over the Tabernacle. He didn't just want to see it on Moses, he wanted to feel and know and sense it for himself.

2. JOSHUA WAS A WARRIOR SERVANT

Our first introduction to Joshua in Scripture was on the battlefield. He appears as Moses' warrior, fighting Amalek at Rephidim.[4]

"So Joshua did as Moses had said to him, and fought with Amalek" Exodus 17:10

---

3   Joshua 1:5
4   Exodus 17:8-16

His first appearance is one of a trusted warrior submitted to his general Moses. This first great battle is considered by the Lord one of great "memorial" to be recorded in a book. This is no insignificant battle led by a young and loyal general. Yet, this young general, mighty in war, is called Moses' minister.

> *"And Moses rose up, and his minister Joshua"*
> Exodus 24:13

The Hebrew word sharath (minister) means, "to serve (as a menial person or worshipper), to attend, to wait on, to do service"[5]. It was the service provided by royal household workers.

Joshua learned servanthood. Most of the great giant killers I have met around the world have learned servanthood. It is one of the great foundation stones for a giant killer. Joshua could wage serious war as a champion under Moses direction or he could wash Moses clothes or polish his shoes.

3. JOSHUA WAS THOROUGHLY MENTORED

Joshua is one of the great examples in Scripture of a man diligently mentored and thoroughly prepared for the task ahead.

Moses was given clear instruction from God concerning his servant and successor Joshua.

> *"But charge Joshua, and encourage him, and strengthen him: for he shall go over before this people, and he shall cause them to inherit the land which thou shalt see."*
> Deuteronomy 3: 28

Moses was given instruction to do three things in Joshua's life: charge, encourage and strengthen him.

---

5   Strong's H8334

Here is our instruction to the giant killers we are mentoring.

1. <u>Charge</u> - the Hebrew word tsavah[6] has a few meanings. Strong's tell us that it means, " make firm, establish, ordain or commission (set apart), delegate and on a human level is the instruction of a father to a son."

There is a great parallel with the instruction and fatherly handling by Paul of the young man Timothy.

In 2 Timothy, Paul on death row in Rome, exhorts and charges a young, frightened pastor Timothy who is facing tremendous persecution. As we read his strong but loving words to the young man he refers to as his "beloved son", we sense the same fatherly strength that Moses injected into the young man Joshua.

Paul has laid hands on young Timothy, imparting gifts, setting him apart and ordaining him as his successor at the great church at Ephesus. Moses had indeed laid his hands upon Joshua[7] to set him apart to lead a nation.

It is important for us to set apart those we mentor, by laying hands on them and praying for a spiritual impartation of gifts and abilities.

> *"Wherefore I put thee in remembrance that thou stir up the gift of God, which is in thee by the putting on of my hands."* 2 Timothy 1:6

Future giant killers need to be nurtured, exhorted, prayed over and strongly encouraged.

2. <u>Encourage</u> – The Hebrew word chazaq[8] means, "to strengthen, build resolve and make courageous and valiant." It means, "to invest a conquering spirit, to make firm and to build resolve." The word encourage simply means to in-courage or to bring into courage.

---

6   Strong's H6680
7   Numbers 27:18-23
8   Strong's H2388

What a charge was given to Moses. God calls him by encouragement to forge Joshua into a strong, valiant man with a conquering resolve. This is the challenge to the body of Christ.

Paul encouraged Timothy by assuring him that he knew the mighty faith that dwelt in his mother and grandmother and of his certainty that the same powerful faith dwelt in him also. He assured Timothy that God had not given him "the spirit of fear"[9] but a "spirit of power". The word for power is dunamis in the Greek language. He urged Timothy to push on as a hardened soldier with a sound, renewed mind.

Paul's words to Timothy are charges, encouragement and words of strength.

3. <u>Strengthen</u> – The Hebrew word 'amats[10] means, "to be alert, courageous, steadfastly minded, hardened, prevailing and obstinate."

These are the characteristics that God required Moses to implant and impart into his young apprentice. As I consider this I am reminded of Paul's powerful final instructions to the church at Ephesus.

"Finally, my brethren, be strong in the Lord, and in the power of his might. Put on the whole armour of God, that ye may be able to stand against the wiles of the devil. For we wrestle not against flesh and blood, but against principalities, against powers, against the rulers of the darkness of this world, against spiritual wickedness in high places. Wherefore take unto you the whole armour of God, that ye may be able to withstand in the evil day, and having done all, to stand." Ephesians 6: 10-13

The charges of Moses to Joshua and Paul to Timothy are the same that we are to build into those we are mentoring.

Moses urged Joshua again and again to be "strong and very courageous"[11].

---

9   II Timothy 1:7
10   Strong's H553
11   Joshua 1:7a

Encouragement is so vital to us all. I thank God for the encouragement I received from my father. As a keen sportsman, I was always keen to perform well. Whenever I saw my father in the crowd, I grew on the inside and felt a sense of confidence and certainty. Moses certainly built this into Joshua. He laid hands on him to impart a spirit of wisdom.[12] He even took him part of the way up to the presence of God, as he ascended the mountain that was aflame with God's glory.[13]

Moses changed his name from Hoshea (salvation) to Joshua (Jehovah is my salvation).[14]

After he had mentored and trained Joshua for years, Moses declared that God would be with him as he had been with him. He then gave him five clear instructions:

1. ...be strong and very courageous.[15]
2. ...be careful to do according to all the law.[16]
3. ...do not turn to the right or the left...[17]
4. ...meditate on it (word) day and night.[18]
5. This book of the law shall not depart from thy mouth...[19]

JOSHUA WAS A MAN OF THE WORD

Constantly he waited on God for His word with regards to strategy for battle. He did not go into action until the word was clear. He commanded his men to do according to the word[20]. He rehearsed and read the law and the promises of God to his men.

---

12   Deuteronomy 34:9
13   Exodus 24:13-18
14   Numbers 13:8,16
15   Joshua 1:7
16   Joshua 1:7
17   Joshua 1:7
18   Joshua 1:8
19   Joshua 1:8
20   Joshua 3:9

"And afterward he read all the words of the law, the blessings and cursings, according to all that is written in the book of the law. There was not a word of all that Moses commanded, which Joshua read not before all the congregation of Israel,..." Joshua 8:34, 35

Here is our great challenge as giant killers: to walk in a place of dependence on the word of God.

JOSHUA WAS A MAN OF DETAIL

Joshua believed in diligence. The spies were continually sent to gain complete understanding of the opposition, terrain and logistics required for battle. History reveals diligent generals and those who went into battle that failed to assess their situation. Napoleon Bonaparte was so thorough that he had studied the maps and charts over and over until he had exhausted every possibility and lived the battle for days before a shot was fired. Had it not been for his defeat at Waterloo, he may be seen as possibly the greatest general since Alexander.

The tragic disaster at Gallipoli in 1915 cost at least 40,000 lives. Stephen Weir, in his book History's Worst Decisions, called it a "vainglorious and pointless attack on an impregnable peninsula". Not only were supplies limited, intelligence scant and lacking in assessment of the geographical topography, understanding of defences hopelessly misread but the whole challenge, to invade Turkey by the Dardanelles, was considered, even by Vice-Admiral Carden, as totally reckless.

Troops were landed on the wrong beaches and others were slaughtered by the hundreds as they landed on beaches where the landscape created a perfect killing field for the Turkish defenders.

The homework had simply not been done thoroughly. The results were tragic.

Joshua was thorough in preparation and driven only by the clear word of God.

JOSHUA WAS A MAN OF CONSECRATION AND HOLINESS

As I read the exploits of this warrior of God, as he seized cities and towns by the hundreds when he took the Promised Land, I see a man of total consecration to God. He reveals a consistency of passion for God, a desire to please Him continually and to keep the word of God not just constantly in his mouth but in the heart of Israel.

In him we find no compromise, no timidity and no turning back, only a God-inspired passion to totally fulfil his divine destiny.

He is one of the men of history who completed his task before he finally settled in the city of Timnath-Serah.

To summarise Joshua the giant killer these are his successes:

1. He longed for God's presence.
2. He was truly strong and courageous.
3. He didn't turn to the left or right but went straight for the objective.
4. He kept the word continually in his mouth and before Israel.
5. He planned thoroughly and diligently exercised God's plan.
6. He was continually dependent on the Lord without deviation.
7. He remained consecrated and demanded holiness personally and as a nation.

CALEB

The third giant killer that comes under the microscope is Caleb. He is one of the most inspiring characters in Scripture. He didn't face just one giant but a whole region inhabited by a giant race and controlled by their warrior King, Arba, and three significant warrior giants, Talmai, Sheshan and Ahiman. What makes Caleb unusual is that his attack and great victory came in his mid to late 80s. He was still savage in battle and totally invincible as he neared 90-years-old.

> *"Forty years old was I when Moses the servant of the Lord sent me from Kadeshbarnea to espy out the land; and I brought him word again as it was in mine heart. Nevertheless my brethren that went up with me made the heart of the people melt: but I wholly followed the Lord my God.*
> *And Moses sware on that day, saying, Surely the land whereon thy feet have trodden shall be thine inheritance, and thy children's for ever, because thou hast wholly followed the Lord my God.*
> *And now, behold, the Lord hath kept me alive, as he said, these forty and five years, even since the Lord spake this word unto Moses, while the children of Israel wandered in the wilderness: and now, lo, I am this day fourscore and five years old.*
> *As yet I am as strong this day as I was in the day that Moses sent me: as my strength was then, even so is my strength now, for war, both to go out, and to come in. Now therefore give me this mountain, whereof the Lord*

spake in that day; for thou heardest in that day how the Anakims were there, and that the cities were great and fenced: if so be the Lord will be with me, then I shall be able to drive them out, as the Lord said.

And Joshua blessed him, and gave unto Caleb the son of Jephunneh Hebron for an inheritance.

Hebron therefore became the inheritance of Caleb the son of Jephunneh the Kenezite unto this day, because that he wholly followed the Lord God of Israel.

And the name of Hebron before was Kirjath arba; which Arba was a great man among the Anakims. And the land had rest from war."

Joshua 14: 7-15

WHO SAID I'M TOO OLD?

The old leathery-skinned champion stood before General Joshua. They had watched a whole generation of unbelieving warriors die in the parched desert of the Sinai Peninsula. The twelve men sent in to spy the Promised Land were leaders, warriors and men of reputation and renown, yet ten died having never fulfilled or seized their God-given destiny. They were stopped by the intimation of giants. What a contrast was God's old gladiator!

Caleb's body at the age of 85 was still muscled and sinewed. He looked like he had just stepped out of the gym. He had that look that was coined in Vietnam: "the eye of the tiger". His eyes gleamed with a glint of anticipation and confidence as he approached Joshua. This is my version of his words uttered with strength and purpose:

> "I am 85-years-old today and as strong as I was at 40. I can travel through any desolate condition you could name and fight any warrior I should confront. I am an 85-year-old warrior, a 'violent man' of 'intense exertion' and 'ardent zeal' and ready to seize by violent assault my prize and inheritance, give me my mountain that God promised me."

TIM HALL

"NOW THEREFORE GIVE ME THIS MOUNTAIN WHEREOF THE LORD SPAKE IN THAT DAY"[1]

His burning God-given vision kept him vitally alive, youthfully fit and full of manly courage and resolve.

"I want this mountain!" shouted the old warrior. Of all the land that could be chosen, why this mountain? What was its great significance to the 85-year-old general? It seemed very personal to Caleb. It was possibly the toughest region to seize, as it was ruled over by the chief giant Arba with powerful, fortified, walled cities. Caleb seemed unable to shake its place from his mind. What was its historical relevance?

This mountain Kirjatharba or Hebron is one of the most significant locations in Old Testament history. The name in Hebrew means "city of the four giants"[2] or "city of Arba" (chief of the giants of the region).

MOUNTAIN OF HEROES

This mountain was the burial place of Caleb's heroes. Here, his nation had been born through the heroics of daring and unrelenting obedience and faith.

This was the place where the legends of faith had walked, lived and ultimately chosen as their final resting place.

Kirjatharba was Abraham's place of destiny. Abraham left his home in Ur of the Chaldees to take his city whose foundation was of God. He had chosen to live here.

Caleb could see the great foundations upon which he would build his destiny. The steps he had taken at 40-years-old were steps in the same place his faith heroes had walked. He wanted to seize back God's mountain of yesterday's faith and establish a new day of faith on the awesome foundation that Abraham and Sarah had laid.

Caleb didn't say to give me Abraham's mountain to relive yesterday. He said, "Give me this mountain", so that I can write my chapter of faith.

1   Joshua 14:12
2   http://en.wikipedia.org/wiki/Kiryat_Arba

70

Certainly, giants roamed the region that had been claimed for the people of God. This seemed to make it more tantalising to Caleb.

This was, for him, a whole new era with a whole new generation of conquerors.

Caleb desperately wanted the established faith foundation on which to build his future. He wanted this, the mountain of his heroes, on which to establish his part in history.

Abraham had, so long before, purchased a small block of land and a cave, which was a small beginning. Caleb now seized the entire mountain region in a mighty, fearless campaign of demonstrated faith. Abraham left a memorial of inspired faith. Caleb would take it to fulfilment.

> *"These all died in faith, not having received the promises, but having seen them afar off, and were persuaded of them, and embraced them..."* Hebrews 11:13

Abraham had seen the fulfilment from a long distance and was persuaded of the future. He embraced with certain faith a great day of triumph. Caleb had seen this day from a distance also and was persuaded of his day. He embraced its certainty and he seized it with passionate resolve. He fulfiled what Abraham had glimpsed. He was grafted in to Abraham's vision. We are also grafted into Abraham's vision.

> *"...So shall thy seed be."* Genesis 15:5b

As I looked over thousands of new converts during one of our South Pacific crusades, God spoke to me:

> **"Don't you know that you are grafted into Abraham? These are the fulfilment of some of the stars Abraham saw that night when I said 'So shall your seed be'."**

TIM HALL

WHAT IS MY MOUNTAIN?

From the time that I found Christ I walked, in my mind and spirit, the mountain of my faith heroes. On the screen of my heart I walked the miracle mountain trod by Smith Wigglesworth. I could hear his broad Yorkshire brogue shouting, "e's 'ealed!" as cancer victims and cripples jumped and leaped. I walked in my mind the great auditoriums of the USA with Kathryn Kuhlman as dozens of wheelchairs were emptied because of the great anointing that she carried. In my mind and heart I walked the mountain of the great Welsh revival with Evan Roberts. I sensed that divine convicting fire that caused grown men to crash to their knees to beg for the Saviour's grace. I walked with Maria Woodworth Etter at the turn of the last century. I could see in my mind this 1.2 m (4 feet 11 inch) woman of God supernaturally frozen in St Louis, Missouri for three days. I could see tens of thousands of people swarming into the stadium to see this wonder and then to experience the engulfing miracle power that healed thousands and saw them ushered into living faith with Christ during this raw display of God's power.

As I read extraordinary stories of John G. Lake, the apostle to Africa, I walked onto his mountain. I could hear him shout, "Let the lightning fire of God burn out the cancer from Hell!" I could feel the awe of the multitudes as miracles exploded on every side. I could see the 700,000 people established into churches in South Africa.

I could see one third of England saved as John Wesley and George Whitfield roamed their mountain of faith. I could see Charles G. Finney shake the East coast of the United States with an estimated 500,000 people who found Christ in one year.

THIS WAS THEIR MOUNTAIN

I want that awesome anointing upon my life. I want every step that I take for God to be alive with the power that Wigglesworth, Lake or Kuhlman carried but I want to carry it into my day and to build on their foundations.

Today, we are watching with awe the great preachers and church statesmen building their mountains on the foundations established by past generations. The impact is greater and more explosive than ever in our history.

Caleb desperately wanted to seize that place of memorial and vision of his heroes but he didn't intend to relive Abraham's faith. This was his faith, his God ordained moment of conquest.

Yesterday was vital to his tomorrow. But his desperate desire was to write a new chapter using Abraham's mountain as the launching pad into his destiny.

Kirjatharba will never be known as Abraham's mountain. It will always be known as Caleb's mountain. It is recalled as Caleb's demonstration of faith and valour.

Kirjatharba will always be remembered for an 85-year-old giant killer who seized and established his place in God's great eternal plan. It will be recalled as the mountain where Abraham dwelt but Caleb conquered, preparing it as the holy place where their king would be crowned. It will be remembered as the place where an 85-year-old warrior drove off and killed the giants who sought to rule God's mountain.

This is your day: the day when you will write your own chapter of history; the day when your exploits will overshadow those of your heroes. Some day, young men and women will read of your exploits, your mountains taken, your giants slain, only to cry out to God, "Give me my mountain!"

AGE IS OVERRATED

Age is certainly a very overrated issue in the Body of Christ. Moses, our first mentioned giant killer, was launched into his great ministry at 80-years-old. His defeat of Og of Bashan occurred after he was 100-years-old and, at his death at the age of 120, we read that, "His eye was not dim, nor his natural force abated."[3]

---

3   Deuteronomy 34:7

Joshua's great, giant conquering impact came in his late 80s like Caleb. Later, we will read that King David was still out fighting the last remnant of giants in his very old age.

It is amazing that the first three great giant killers in Scripture were all over 85-years-old at the peak of their impact, while the next giant killer we consider was only a teenager when he felled the Philistine champion Goliath.

God is far less concerned about age than we are. I don't think God sees our age but He sees our passion, our dreams, our spiritual tenacity and our hunger for Him.

> *"But they that wait upon the LORD shall renew their strength; they shall mount up with wings as eagles; they shall run, and not be weary; and they shall walk, and not faint."*
> Isaiah 40:31

> *"Who satisfieth thy mouth with good things; so that thy youth is renewed like the eagle's."*
> Psalm 103:5

Don't ever let your age, or people's opinion of your age, hold you back or stifle your dreams. Giant killers are not known for their age but their exploits.

"GIVE ME THIS MOUNTAIN!"

Caleb did not want someone else's inheritance. He wanted what God had promised him. He did not envy or try to seize another man's possession.

He was not interested in the inheritance of another tribe or family. He wanted his region of promise. He would run his race, not the race allotted to someone else. He wanted the race that God had set for him. He wanted to fulfil the blueprint God had established for his life before even the foundation of the Earth. It is an incredible thought that the

God of Eternity had a blueprint for your life and mine before the day of creation. God had prepared mountains that we would take and knew the awesome giants that would oppose us as we grew as eternal warriors in God's great faith arena.

> *"Wherefore seeing we also are compassed about with so great a cloud of witnesses, let us lay aside every weight, and the sin which doth so easily beset us, and let us run with patience the race that is set before us."*
> Hebrews 12:1

CALEB NEVER LOST SIGHT OF HIS DESTINY

Kirjatharba, the city of Arba, was a mountain stronghold controlled by four giants, with Arba as the awesome warrior chief. It was a beautiful but foreboding mountain region with massively fortified cities, controlled by a barbaric giant race who roamed the region to destroy strangers or enemies dared enter their domain.

When we step out in the purpose of God, often it seems like we've stepped into Kirjatharba. It is like stepping into a realm or dimension where we are most unwelcome. Some years ago, I heard Dr David Yonggi Cho from Korea describe the horrors that confronted him as they built what was then the largest church building in the world. Financial and other pressures became so overwhelming during the process that he walked onto the edge of his building to commit suicide. Then he remembered a very important appointment and thus postponed the suicide for a later time. Thank God that he faced and overcame those giants of his Kirjatharba and that he has impacted the world with his Caleb-like tenacity. Thank God the giant did not succeed but fell before another man of prayer, vision and resolve.

Caleb's feet had walked these mountains of Kirjatharba 45 years before. The bones of the patriarchs were buried there. His nostrils had been filled with the smell of its foliage as he gazed out over this majestic place that God said was his. He had felt the sun, warm on his face, and felt the breezes blowing around him. He had been engulfed with an overwhelming and unshakeable certainty that this was his mountain and no matter how long it took, no matter what giant he would confront or what fortification would try to block his way, he would have his destiny. For 45 years, since that day, he had anticipated the time when he would walk in and take possession of his dream.

As an unbelieving generation had wandered without reason or purpose in a windswept Sinai Peninsula, his mountain was ever before his eyes, in his dreams, in his words and consumed his soul.

As this unbelieving, stiff-necked generation died one after another and their bones parched the desert sands, his eyes sparkled and gleamed with purpose and desire. Nothing could rob him of his destiny. The giants of unbelief, cynicism, fear and death that confronted him continually through the murmuring and defeated attitude of everyone about him could not stifle his dream.

He had never lost sight of the mountain that he knew was his. His God-breathed dream had kept vitality and strength filling his soul. The Promised Land was his. He would not be shaken. His vision had kept him young, vital and filled with youthful anticipation.

A whole generation, with him for 40 years, stumbled through a mundane and aimless existence, but Caleb saw, smelled and felt his destiny. His heart pounded with destiny, purpose and challenge. The wilderness did not claim him, nor did his bones parch the desert sands. He claimed his destiny. When it happened or how old physically he was, mattered not. He saw his dream fulfilled.

HOW MUCH DO YOU WANT YOUR DESTINY?

Caleb's name means "forcible or attacking dog"[4]. This certainly was his nature. He was not shaken as he desperately and tenaciously pushed towards his unchanging dream. No giant that rose up intimidated him.

It is hard to imagine how devastated Caleb was when ten warrior

---

4   Strong's H3612

leaders melted like "grasshoppers" and chose death in the desert rather than their God-given inheritance.

How often do we see men and women of God, with great destinies ahead, "fully armed turn back in the day of battle"? May we never be included in the group who "shrink back" and cause no pleasure in the heart of God.

Certainly Jebusites, Hittites and giants roamed the land but hadn't God promised this land to Abraham?[5]

This was their God-given destiny, the inheritance for them and their families.

Caleb must have groaned and squirmed as the ten declared to Moses, "your little ones…should be a prey".[6]

Moses must have shaken his head in astonishment. After they saw the Egyptian army swallowed up in the sea by the mighty judgment of God and demonstration of His power, they turned away. Surrender in war must be a soul-destroying thing. I have studied the surrender of the Allied Forces in Singapore during World War II and always cringe when I consider such a meek response to an opportunity that should have stopped Japan's advance into the South Pacific.

The insipid failure of God's people to grasp the Promised Land within ten days is pitiful.

> *"Yea, they turned back and tempted God, and limited the Holy One of Israel."* Psalm 78:41

The ten spies may have seen themselves as grasshoppers but Caleb boldly barked out like a wild dog:

> *"Only rebel not ye against the LORD, neither fear ye the people of the land; for they are bread for us: their defence is departed from them, and the LORD is with us: fear them not."* Numbers 14:9

---

5   Genesis 15:18-21
6   Numbers 14:31

He saw the giants and warriors as bread, as "the breakfast of champions".

Caleb's voice must have been a warrior's roar: "They are bread for us!" They are there to be devoured, swallowed up. Their defence is "departed...and the Lord is with us". What can possibly stop us? With God's hand on our lives, God's word in our mouth and God's plan and direction in our heart and steps, surely we can boldly declare as we face our Kirjatharbas:

"They are bread to us and those defences, strong as they may seem, are already departed and melted before us."

CALEB SAW GIANTS AS "THE BREAKFAST OF CHAMPIONS"[7]

Rick Godwin from San Antonio, USA boldly declared, "The giants we face in the quest for our mountain are 'the breakfast of champions'". They are there to be devoured. It is interesting that in 2 Samuel 21:15, when David and his mighty men went down against the four giants and the Philistine host, the word "fought against" in the Hebrew is well translated "devoured" or "consumed"[8].

WHERE ARE THOSE GIANTS NOW?

Ask any man or woman, who has passionately seized the awesome inheritance that God had prepared for them, whether they confronted giants and walled cities. Ask them if they had confronted huge giants that cast shadows of doubt, fear and despair over everything they attempted. Ask them if giants sought out their children as prey or targeted their marriages or assaulted their finances. Ask them if walled cities rose up in their path as massive roadblocks. Ask them if giants sought their health, troubled their minds and emotions or buffeted them as spectres in the night.

Ask those who have seized their destiny, taken their God-given

---

7   Rick Godwin

8   Strong's H3898

inheritance if they had confronted giants, "Jebusites", "Amorites" and "Hittites", fierce and vicious opponents in so many different forms. Ask them if there had been a huge cost, great challenges and seemingly impossible obstacles set in their paths.

But ask them, "Where are those giants now? Where is their defiance and intimidation?" It has been swallowed up by the appetite and jaws of relentless, violent faith, zeal and intense exertion. It has been devoured as bread as the "breakfast of champions".

My friend, breakfast is served!

CALEB WAS A MAN OF DESPERATE PASSION

Some years ago, I was again sitting under the ministry of the great Korean apostle, Dr David Yongii Cho. With strength pulsing in his words, I heard him declare, "If you have a vision from God, if necessary die with it, but don't let go." This was certainly Caleb's nature.

One of my farming friends had a Staffordshire Bull Terrier that would seize on to something so ferociously that it was virtually impossible to prise him loose. I am told, on one occasion, the dog leapt up and seized hold of a cow by the shoulder. The cow ran off with the dog firmly attached bouncing about but refusing to let go. This was Caleb's attitude. He had seen, tasted and grasped his destiny and now, like the Staffordshire Bull Terrier, he seized his dream and nothing could shake it from him.

CAN YOU SEE, FEEL AND TASTE YOUR MOUNTAIN?
DOES IT CONSUME YOUR THOUGHTS AND DREAMS?

- What is your God-given inheritance?
- Have you walked on it?
- Have you seen it on the screen of your spirit?
- Have you tasted it and breathed it?

- Does it consume and influence all your decisions and plans?
- Does it cause within you a passion to pray and seize God with a hunger and thirst that cannot be satiated or satisfied?
- Does it push you through a wilderness such that your eyes still gleam and sparkle with the intensity that only vision can produce?
- Does it cause you to stand tall and unbending when those around you give up and shrink back?
- Does it drive you through inner barriers or fears?
- Does it push you forcibly beyond the words of doubt, intimidation and unbelief that so often strike like the carrion of hell?

YOU HAVEN'T WANTED THESE THINGS BADLY ENOUGH

Recently, I was in prayer, considering areas that I felt I should have achieved by this time of my life. I asked the Lord why some of these things had not yet come to pass. I wondered why I had not broken through into areas of dreams and visions that I had received many years ago. His words came strongly into my spirit:

"You haven't wanted these things badly enough."

How badly do you want to seize the dreams that God has put in your heart? How determined are you that nothing can or will hinder your progress?

I have learned over years of ministry that God has made it so that we must pursue Him and earnestly desire Him and His presence. He informs us that those who diligently search after Him will find Him.[9] I believe that prayer is God's gift to man that enables him to explore the vast expanses of His glorious unlimited nature and power.

God's giant killers know what their mountain is and their hearts are set to seize their God-given inheritance.

Jesus said in Mark 11:24:

9   Jeremiah 29:13

*"...What things soever ye desire, when ye pray, believe
that ye receive them, and ye shall have them."*

The word "desire"[10] is a strong word with the sense of craving after,
even lusting after.

For 40 years in the wilderness, Caleb craved the mountain he had
walked upon. The promise consumed and drove him, pushing him
through every obstacle that the enemy could use to block him.

Nothing could stop God's aged gladiator. No wonder God said he
had "another spirit"[11], an indomitable, unstoppable, insatiable attitude
that could not be shaken.

Giant killers and mountain takers must have another spirit, a
spirit of conquest and daring tenacity, unshakeable by life's strongest
tempests.

GIANT OF DOUBLE MINDEDNESS

Caleb knew his race with all of its challenges and obstacles. He
had visualised it, contemplated and been consumed by it for 40 long
years of wandering in the Sinai Desert surrounded by the unbelieving
generation who had stifled and prevented his destiny.

Too often people are frustrated as they watch other people pursuing
and obtaining the mountain of their dreams while they flounder with
uncertainty in the confusion of double mindedness.

Double mindedness is a real giant to be confronted. No matter how
skilled or talented a person may be, double mindedness will prevent
him from ever taking his objectives.

Over many years of ministry, I have enjoyed pioneering churches,
pastoring, conducting seminars and conferences but my deepest
passion is to stand on big outdoor stages preaching to seas of humanity
and watching thousands finding Christ and miraculously healed.

As an evangelist, life is far less certain (especially financially) than as
the pastor of a thriving church. The constant challenge of raising large

10   Strong's G154
11   Numbers 14:24

amounts of finance to conduct crusades and living on that constant faith edge causes many evangelists to take on a pastorate where there is a regular wage and security for their family.

I have enjoyed pioneering and pastoring churches during 35 years of ministry and have had some good success but I have had a constant pull of God for crusade evangelism.

Ps Rick Shelton (Joyce Meyer's former pastor) once told me that a baseball or cricket bat has a sweet spot. This is the part of the bat that when the ball is hit, it seems to be the perfect spot for distance and comfort of impact. He said that as ministers, for fulfilment of our destiny, we must find the area of gifting that is our "sweet spot". He said, for him it is pastoring and building a great church. I know, for me it is travelling the world releasing the supernatural power of God. For others it is a combination of both.

We must find the "sweet spot" and then single-mindedly charge this objective for our life.

If Satan can keep Christians in the state of double mindedness, he already has them defeated. Napoleon Bonaparte said:

"Hesitation and half measures lose all in war."[12]

James wrote:
"…let him ask in faith, nothing wavering. For he that wavereth is like a wave of the sea driven with the wind and tossed. For let not that man think that he shall receive any thing of the Lord. A double minded man is unstable in all his ways." James 1:6-8

If the giants of life can keep us in a place where we vacillate[13] in our calling, unsure if we should be pastoring, evangelising or making money for the Kingdom, we will be kept in a place of total instability. This is a place where even God cannot bless our plans. God is a precise

12   http://www.napoleon-series.org/research/napoleon/c_quotes.html
13   Vacillate, 1.To waver in mind or opinion; be indecisive or irresolute. "His tendency to vacillate makes him a poor leader." 2. To sway unsteadily; waver; totter; stagger.. 3.To oscillate or fluctuate.

God of detail and pattern.

Until we have clearly determined what our mountain is, we run uncertainly without real aim. We must clearly, passionately and aggressively establish (through prayer) our goals, plans and purposes and "run with endurance the race that is set before us".[14]

> The Apostle Paul said:
> *"Not as though I had already attained, either were already perfect: but I follow after, if that I may apprehend that for which also I am apprehended of Christ Jesus. Brethren, I count not myself to have apprehended: but this one thing I do, forgetting those things which are behind, and reaching forth unto those things which are before, I press toward the mark for the prize of the high calling of God in Christ Jesus."* Philippians 3:12-14

Paul knew his target and divine call and ruthlessly pursued it.

DOUBLE MINDEDNESS IS ONE OF THE GREATEST GIANTS THAT STOPS US FROM CLEARLY DEFINING OUR GOALS AND FEROCIOUSLY PURSUING THEM

> *"I therefore so run, not as uncertainly; so fight I, not as one that beateth the air"* 1 Corinthians 9:26

In the famous British comedy series Monty Python's Flying Circus, one skit featured an Olympic running event for runners with "no sense of direction". When the starter's gun fired, each of the dozen or so runners took off in totally different directions. It reminded me of churches that I've seen. So often in churches, everyone seems to be pursuing his own direction and then wondering why the church doesn't grow.

A good leader who has heard from God will gather his church

14   Hebrews 12:1 NKJV

together passionately in a single direction.

Rick Warren's remarkable books The Purpose Driven Life and the The Purpose Driven Church have impacted the world. A life or church can only be purpose driven when it clearly knows its direction and purpose.

Paul knew his call and pursued it like a hunter stalking his prey. He clearly knew his reason for walking on the earth and hungrily pushed through every obstacle to fulfil his heavenly vision.

When we have clearly come to know what our mountain is, we can run purposefully and desperately and clearly the incredible race that is ours. Single mindedness is a vital key to the seizing of our destiny.

We must clearly establish from God what our mountain is and then single-mindedly pursue it like Caleb of old.

CALEB'S BURNING VISION KEPT HIM PHYSICALLY YOUNG AND VIBRANT

"As yet I am as strong this day as I was in the day that Moses sent me: as my strength was then, even so is my strength now, for war, both to go out, and to come in."
Joshua 14:11

Amazingly Caleb's strength had not abated in 85 years. This is not, as some would say, his spiritual strength. This is his physical and mental strength to scale cliffs, cross rivers in flood with full pack and armour, fight 3 m (10 feet) tall giants, wield sword and buckler through days of battle and route march 30 miles per day. These are the words of an 85-year-old man who is still in peak physical condition and hungry for conquest.

The Hebrew word translated as "strong" means "hard" (physically)[15], while the word translated as "strength" means "firm, vigorous, capable, and full of hardiness and power."[16] This is a powerful testimony for an 85-year-old man.

---

15   Strong's H2389
16   Strong's H3581

"But they that wait upon the Lord shall renew their strength; they shall mount up with wings as eagles; they shall run, and not be weary; and they shall walk, and not faint." Isaiah 40:31

What was the key to Caleb's vitality? He ate the same food and drank the same drink that the nation had shared in the wilderness. He had walked the same road of soul-sapping hardship yet he remained resolute, resilient, and totally optimistic. He was surrounded by the nation of Israel that God called:

"...this evil congregation, which murmur against me"
Numbers 14:27

Despite the incessant murmuring and pessimistic negativity that surrounded him every day in the wilderness, he emerged defiant, resilient, physically youthful and passionate, ready for conquest with giants.
- He didn't see desert sand. He saw mountain grandeur.
- He didn't see giants. He saw milk, honey and unspeakable prosperity.
- He didn't see death in the desert sand. He saw a long life lived out in an awesome inheritance for himself, his family and his nation.

His eyes were focussed totally on the Promised Land, not on the giants and his dream kept him vital, youthful, motivated and physically strong. His focus was correct. Where is your focus? Is it on your mountain or the difficulties that confront you?

"Where there is no vision, the people perish"
Proverbs 29:18

OUR DREAMS KEEP US YOUNG AND VITALLY STRONG

Why is it that so many fit and vital men, after reaching retiring age and ceasing work, are soon dead? Man is born to dream dreams, to see visions, to plan projects and conquests. A person is only as young as the dreams that consume him. Renewed strength and vitality are gifts of God. When a person no longer has a purpose or dream in life, he has entered old age.

We are never too old to dream dreams, to plan ventures, to invent, to build, to conquer, to inspire. Remember Moses was living in total vitality at 120-years-old after 40 tough years of stress, disappointment and war that started at 80-years-old. The previous 40 years had been lived as an exile.

His constant vision of the Promised Land shared by Joshua and Caleb kept these men as the most ferocious warriors on earth with over 290 years' life experience between them.

The holy vision consumed Caleb as he took God one hundred percent at His word. The most powerful thing that we can possess, outside of salvation and the mighty baptism in the Holy Ghost, is a supernatural dream and strategy planted in our being by the overshadowing and brooding power of the most high God.

DREAMERS SHAPE HISTORY

History has been, and continues to be, shaped and changed by dreamers and visionaries. The great generals and conquerors of history were all consumed by a dream. As we study these men who led great armies into conquest of the nations, we see their dreams driving them on.

ALEXANDER THE GREAT

Alexander of Macedonia, known universally as Alexander the Great, is considered by many historians to have been the greatest general in military history. His skill and genius impacted Julius Caesar, Napoleon, Lord Nelson, emperors and generals throughout history.

Alexander was trained by his father Philip for global conquest from childhood.

He was born in 356BC to King Philip of Northern Macedonia, who was almost certainly the most advanced military mind who had ever lived up to this time. His skill in war, as he cleverly designed and built battle and siege implements, understood of supply lines and trained of crack soldiers, especially cavalry, set him apart as totally unique on earth.

His son Alexander had so impressed Philip from an early age that he built his philosophy of life and conquest into him. At 13-years-old, young Alexander made an indelible mark on his father's view of him.

At a horse sale, Philip had noted with interest a massive black horse that could not be handled or tamed by anyone. The horse seemed beyond control, until young Alexander left his father's side, took the bridle and turned the great beast about. He rode it to his father who stood in stunned pride and disbelief.

Alexander noticed the horse's fear of its own shadow, so he turned him into the sun and mounted him.

According to Plutarch, the first century Greek historian, Philip turned to his son weeping with joy, and said:

"My boy you must find a kingdom big enough for your ambition. Macedonia is too small for you."
Arrian, the second century Roman Historian

Fierce, ambitious, unwavering in his own self belief and fuelled by a deep sense that he was divinely blessed, protected and watched over by the gods, he was convinced of divine purpose. He felt set apart by the gods to his great global campaigns. Within him burnt a certainty that he was set apart to not just seize Persia but to bring change to the world. His global impact, militarily and culturally, has been felt ever since.

How prophetic would Philip's word be?

Following his father's assassination, Alexander barely 20-years-old, began a conquest that saw the known world seized in less than a decade. He led his men into battle continually – always mounted on the great horse, Bucephelus, which he had mastered at 13-years-old.

In one short decade, this young general, who began with an army of 35,000 fine Macedonian warriors, seized the known world: Persia, Greece, the Middle East, Afghanistan, today's Pakistan and much of India. The known world fell to the young visionary Macedonian king whose daring, self belief, unswerving vision, tactical brilliance, inspirational genius and indomitable courage made him the greatest military general in history.

Alexander dripped with vision from the moment he set his goal to seize Persia, crush Darius and take Babylon and make it his city.

Just prior to his death at the age of 30, he wept in despair that there remained, "no more kingdoms to conquer".

At just 30-years-old he conquered the greatest part of the known world and brought change like no man who had ever lived up to that point in time.

His inner dreams were backed by powerful personality traits that every giant slaying dreamer should possess.

Alexander's great dreams, and courageous passion to achieve them, remind me of the extraordinary character Caleb.

Alexander inspired and motivated all around him by the scale of his dream and the enormous personal courage he showed as he brought his dreams to pass.

Arrian, the second century Roman historian, gives us real insight into the great general of antiquity. This was the statement about Alexander made by Ptolemy his general at Ephesus. In it, we sense his unshakeable optimism in battle.

He had invincible power of endurance and a keen intellect; he was brave and adventurous…and hungry for fame. He had an uncanny instinct for the right course in a difficult and complex situation. In arming, equipping troops and in his military dispositions, he was masterly.

Noble indeed was his power of inspiring his men, of filling them with confidence and in the moment of danger, of sweeping away their fear by the spectacle of his own fearlessness. When risks had to be taken, he took them with utmost boldness and his ability to settle the moment for a swift blow, before the enemy had any suspicion of what was coming was beyond praise.[17]

In these words, we can sense an infectious boldness that caused men to grow on the inside to achieve great feats in battle.

I sense that the above quote well describes the impact of David as he raised up his mighty men.

The Bible tells us that Caleb had "another spirit".

CALEB HAD AN AUDACIOUS INDOMITABLE SPIRIT: GIANT KILLERS ARE PREPARED TO DO AUDACIOUS THINGS

"But my servant Caleb, because he had another spirit with him, and hath followed me fully, him will I bring into the land whereinto he went; and his seed shall possess it." Numbers 14:24

"Wild dog, audacious, ferocious", certainly describes the character of Caleb. He didn't consider the size of the giants of Kirjatharba. Instead, he contemplated the thrust of his sword cutting down these controllers of his destiny.

Caleb had a born-to-win, audacious attitude, an attitude that couldn't be quenched, discouraged, paralysed or extinguished. This is the attitude we must possess. We must be filled with the certainty of the call of God and a consciousness of the awesome overshadowing supernatural hand of the great God of eternity.

The apostle Paul had this attitude that made him unstoppable.

---

17   Arrian, second century Roman historian, The Campaigns of Alexander.

"Nay, in all these things we are more than conquerors through him that loved us." Romans 8:37

What sets one man apart from another? What is it in the nature of one man that causes him to seize life and destiny with a fury, while others sit back living in mundane ease? Ordinary men rise up to do great things, even men without Christ's power and strength. There is an attitude that varies from life to life.

SHAKA ZULU

The great African general Shaka Zulu reveals something of the attitude that brings an army into victory. His army moved faster than any army in history had previously moved. Here is a quote about him from his Aunt Minkabayi, the great princess of the Zulu nation:

> **"The first order from my nephew to his regiment shocked them. The great thunderer ordered them to take off their sandals and never to wear them again. 'We need to defeat the enemy with speed. Speed is our biggest weapon. Sandals frustrate speed, they slow a man down. Only retired old men must wear sandals.' The great thunderer led from the front when he asked his warriors to discard sandals and stomp out the thorns on the ground, he was the first one to do that. O' yes I remember him dancing and singing as he showed his soldiers how to do it. At first they could not believe their eyes, but on seeing their leader setting the example, they joined in enthusiastically chanting in his honour, 'Sigidi, Sigidi – the hoe that surpasses other hoes in it sharpness!' Yes, as the dust rose, covering the skies, his warriors danced with their leader, totally disregarding the pain and blood from their feet."** [18]

---

18   Shaka Zulu's Aunt Minkabayi, quoted from page 32, Phinda Mzwakhe Madi, Leadership Lessons from Emperor Shaka Zulu the Great, Knowledge Resources, South Africa.

Again, in this general, we see great dreams and unstoppable courage to achieve them.

"Shaka was driven by dreams bigger than the sun..."[19]

Both Alexander the Great and Shaka Zulu achieved enormous things in a few short years before they were cut down as young men. They were also heavily influenced by demonic powers, which ultimately brought about their ruin, but they showed us what was required to conquer nations.

We are of a different spirit with the greatest conquest of history placed before us.

I love the attitude of the great soul-winner Reinhard Bonnke. I heard him make this statement some years ago:

> **"Christians are not the hunted but the hunters; not the attacked but the attackers. We are God's storm troopers sent to release the hostages of hell. We are the invading force of the Lord."** Reinhard Bonnke

I have always found audacity and courageous daring most inspiring. Warfare, although horrendous and hellish, does bring out characteristics that separate soldiers and cause some to stand out in a unique way. One place that has inspired me over the years is the Australian War Museum in Canberra. One room is set apart to commemorate the Victoria Cross winners of our nation. The Victoria Cross is the highest award for valour and features a simple cross forged from melted down cannons from the Crimean War. In this room the exploits of the recipients are outlined. Captured machine guns, medals and descriptions of the exploits of our warriors fill this room. The insignia on the simple but beautiful medal simply says, "FOR VALOUR".

Perhaps my favourite stories of the valour of the Australians at war concerns Albert Jacka, who was later to be Mayor of St Kilda, Melbourne, Australia. At Courtney's Post at Gallipoli, he won Australia's first

---

19   ibid, page 44.

Victoria Cross when he launched himself over a parapet into a trench, shot five Turks, bayoneted two and scattered the rest.

At Pozieres in France, Jacka committed, in the view of A.W. Bean, "the most audacious act of the AIF (Australian Infantry Forces) in World War I." This is the account:

> "At Pozieres on 7th August 1916, the Germans overran a portion of the Australian line that included Jacka's underground dugout. The enemy rolled a bomb into the dugout and wounded two men. Jacka, drawing his revolver, bolted up the stairs and fired at the German bomb-thrower. He found that he and the seven men who joined him were 250 metres behind the German first line. Observing a group of 40 Australian prisoners being escorted by the Germans, he waited until they were within 30 metres before attacking the German guards. A furious hand-to-hand fight ensued in which Jacka was wounded three times, once through the neck. The captured Australians broke away and attacked their captors – men from other units joined in and the tables were turned completely. Most of the Australians broke free. Many Germans were captured and the line was retaken. Jacka received the Military Cross for this action, which Charles Bean described as the most dramatic and effective act of individual audacity in the history of the AIF."

Caleb had a God-given attitude, tenacity and explosive vision. He had a ferocious wild dog attitude.

He truly possessed a different attitude from the ten spies who melted with fear in the Promised Land.

> "...Let us go up at once, and possess it; for we are well able to overcome it."[20]

---

20   Numbers 13:30

"...neither fear ye the people of the land; for they are bread for us: their defence is departed from them, and the LORD is with us: fear them not."[21]

Like the old hardened warrior whose dream never died, passion never wavered and strength didn't wane, let's go after the prize and seize our destiny in the power of the Holy Ghost.

How do we see ourselves? Are we the hunted or the hunters? God sees us, I'm sure, as His "storm troopers set to plunder hell and populate Heaven".

Billy Sunday, the mighty American evangelist of the early 1900's, was a man small in stature, but once declared, "The man on the inside of me is one thousand times larger than the man on the outside."

Caleb was a mountain taker and a giant killer, well described by the writer to the Hebrews in the great "Heroes of Faith" chapter of scripture:

"Who through faith subdued kingdoms, wrought righteousness, obtained promises, stopped the mouths of lions." Hebrews 11: 33

21   Numbers 14:9

CALEB'S CONFESSION WAS UNWAVERING

CALEB NEVER DEVIATED IN HIS DECLARATIONS

Caleb never deviated in his declarations and his confession was clear and concise:

"Let us go up at once"[22]
"Let us possess it"[23]
"We are well able to overcome it"[24]
"Do not fear the people of the land – they are bread for us"[25]
"Their defence is departed from them"[26]
"And the Lord is with us."[27]

Giant killers are declarers of God's promises.

Jesus is called the High Priest of our profession.[28] The Greek work for "profession" or "declaration" is "homologia"[29]; from the words "homo" (the same) and "logos" (the word). Jesus is the High Priest of us saying the same thing. The High Priest is our representative. I picture Jesus going on our behalf to the Father with our declaration and our words.

TESTIMONY OF UNWAVERING CONFESSION

While ministering a great miracle campaign in Honiara in the Solomon Islands, we stayed in a most picturesque hotel built on the side of a huge cliff. The view from the room across Savo Bay was exhilarating. At around sunset, I sat and looked out across the

---

22   Numbers 13:30
23   Numbers 13:30
24   Numbers 13:30
25   Numbers 14:9
26   Numbers 14:9
27   Numbers 14:9
28   Hebrews 4:14
29   Strong's G3671

magnificent Savo Bay. The smell of the Hibiscus and the warm beauty of the place were enchanting. As I laid back and breathed in the atmosphere, I heard a man's voice call my name.

I looked across to the next balcony on my right. The gentleman was from my own city in South Australia.

"I have an incredible testimony to tell you," he declared with sheer enthusiasm.

As I sat in his room a few minutes later, he relayed an extraordinary story to me. It went like this:

He had been diagnosed a year or so before with a large brain tumour. He was a significant business man working with one of Australia's largest insurance companies at the time. The doctor told him that urgent surgery was necessary to save his life. He was also informed that in the process of saving his life, because of the position of the tumour, he would very possibly lose his sight as a result of the operation.

He agreed to the operation, but not until he had gone alone with God to pray through the situation. He went to a beach house to fervently call upon the Lord. He spent several weeks walking the beach and fervently declaring the words of healing from scripture.

Like Caleb he kept declaring his God given inheritance – health and life.

Over and over, he spoke the Word declaring the promises of God. As he kept the Word in front of His eyes and in His mouth, something was happening in his body.

> *"For they (God's words) are life unto those that find them, and health to all their flesh."* Proverbs 4:22

He returned to Adelaide and prepared for surgery. The surgeon explained that, following surgery, his head and eyes would be bandaged and, after a short while, his sight would be assessed.

When he awoke in recovery, after what was to be a long complex operation, his head was bandaged but his sight was perfect.

The surgeon came in to the recovery room, emotional and visibly shaken. He declared that, when they opened the man's skull, they were stunned. A surgeon much superior to them had already operated on the brain, removed the tumour and left sutures so detailed that no surgeon on earth could match His work.

When had God's surgery occurred? Most likely it had taken place as the man walked back and forth on the beach proclaiming the Word of God, confessing and positively declaring the many healing promises of God.

> *"So shall my word be that goeth forth out of my mouth:*
> *it shall not return unto me void, but it shall accomplish*
> *that which I please, and it shall prosper in the thing*
> *whereto I sent it."*
> Isaiah 55:11

This powerful scripture had been declared, confessed and proclaimed continually for two weeks. A mighty miracle of God's grace and power had been performed.

Caleb continued to confess and declare the promise of God. Giant killers proclaim and fearlessly speak the eternal Words of Life. Jesus said:

> *"...the words that I speak unto you, they are spirit, and*
> *they are life."* John 6:63b

Many years ago, I heard the powerful preaching of Pastor Frederick J. Price. He preached about Jesus cursing the fig tree. He talked of the awesome power of our words and the fact that we can move mountains with our words if we dare to believe. The man I spoke with in the hotel in Honiara had seen the removal of a small, but lethal, mountain of death that sought to take his life.

Caleb kept declaring that this mountain was his inheritance, his God-given dwelling and nothing could prevent him from having it.

CONCLUSION

CALEB'S MAIN CHARACTERISTICS

This study of Caleb has shown us certain distinct keys that we can establish in our own lives as we move more deeply into our own Promised Land.

1. Caleb never lost sight of the promise or inheritance.
2. His vision consumed him for 45 years, keeping him physically strong and vibrant.
3. He had no fear of giants. He already saw them as defeated foes, in fact, "bread to be devoured".
4. His declaration was of a one hundred per cent commitment to the God he "wholly followed".
5. He had an indomitable spirit, and was immovable, daring and audacious.

WHAT WAS THE REWARD FOR CALEB'S DESTRUCTION OF THE GIANTS?

"And unto Caleb the son of Jephunneh he gave a part among the children of Judah, according to the commandment of the Lord to Joshua, even the city of Arba the father of Anak, which city is Hebron. And Caleb drove thence the three sons of Anak, Sheshai, and Ahiman, and Talmai, the children of Anak."
Joshua 15:13-14

Kirjatharba, the city of the giants, a place controlled out of Hell became Hebron, "the seat of association" or "fellowship"[30]. It became a Levite city, a place set apart unto the holiness of God and a refuge city for those fleeing for mercy.

Hebron was the Levite city where David, the great giant slaying

---

30   Strong's H2275

king, would later be crowned. For a period of time, it became the capital city of the land.

It is significant that the giant killer David was crowned king on a mountain seized from the hands of the controlling giants.

God's desire for you and me is that we would seize mountain strongholds of satanic control and see them become places that bring absolute glory to God.

5

GOLIATH

"WE WILL BE REMEMBERED FOR THE GIANT WE SLAY OR THE GIANT THAT SLAYS US."[1]

We can learn so much from these giant killers. The last three we looked at were all over 85-years-old, with Moses being over 100. Now, we come to the most famous giant killer in history: a teenager of ruddy complexion who stepped from the work of a shepherd to kingly dominion, David of Bethlehem.

To fully understand the triumph of David as a giant killer, we first need to look at the awesome enemy he faced, Goliath of Gath. Let us look at the scene on that historic day.

The clamour of the Israelite army had suddenly become silent. The giant of Gath had again taken the field. Standing nearly 3.4 m (11 feet) in height, he wore a coat of mail weighing almost 90.7 kg (200 lbs). The head of his massive spear weighed around 9.1 kg (20 lbs). There on the plain of Shochoh, with the sun glinting off his bronze armour, his very appearance sent a shudder through Israel's ranks. His booming, insolent, intimidating voice had echoed through the valley twice per day for 40 days. According to Jewish scholars it was, "to disturb them at the hour set for reciting the Shema (prayer)". His whole demeanour was one of defiance and intimidation. Every day his challenge was the same:

> "...I defy the armies of Israel this day; give me a man, that we might fight together." 1 Samuel 17:10

---

[1] Unknown

When Saul and his army saw and heard him each day they were "dismayed"[2] (broken down, confused, and terrified). They melted at the onslaught of his continual tirade of defiant threats.

He was the champion of Philistia and, according to Jewish history:

> **"[He] boasted of having slain the two sons of Eli, captured the Holy Ark, brought it to Philistia, where it stayed seven months and of having led the van of the Philistines in every war scattering the enemy before him like dust."[3]**

Goliath had no fear of Israel or the God of Israel. He was so full of confidence in battle that he felt himself to be totally invincible.

He had brought down an Israelite army that carried the Ark of God's glory before them. He had slain the guardians of the Ark, the priests Hophni and Phinehas, and carried the Ark away to Dagon's temple. Ignorantly, this giant saw his own great godless strength as the key to the victory not realising that the sinful depravity of the priests, Hophni and Phinehas, Eli's indifference and failure to rectify the situation and Israel's backslidden spiritual state were the real enemies. God had been sorely insulted and had allowed the giant to actually become the instrument of his judgement. Only grievous, sinful indifference had given the giant any place of victory.

According to some Jewish scholars, Goliath carried an image of Dagon, the Philistine god, on his chest armour. It is significant that this giant, like the great stone Philistine god, Dagon[4], who before the Ark of God had crashed face down headless and handless, would later crash face down before God's anointed, David. The champion severed his head of control and took the sword of intimidation as his own personal trophy.

Goliath mentally intimidated and terrorized the Israelite army for 40 days and nights, and paralysed its ranks with his savage presence.

2   I Samuel 17:11
3   www.jewishdictionary.com
4   I Samuel 5:2-7

Rick Renner in his book, Dressed to Kill, said:

> "...It wasn't this weaponry or Goliath's size that caused Israel to shrink back in fear. Then what caused the Israelites to fear? It was the constant threats and mental bombardment that Goliath hit them with every single day. This mental harassment crippled them so that they lost sight of the awesome ability of God."

Intimidation is the major arsenal of the giants we face today, causing us to "lose sight of the awesome ability of God" and see ourselves as grasshoppers in the giant's sight and our own.

GOLIATH MENTALLY AND EMOTIONALLY IMMOBILIZED THE ARMIES OF ISRAEL WITHOUT EVER USING A SWORD OR SPEAR.

> "...With words alone, he incapacitated, disabled, stunned, numbed, and disarmed them. His flagrant and preposterous distortion of his own greatness was so outrageous, that his words bewitched the listening Israelite army until they were spellbound under his verbal control."[5]

Goliath played mind games with backslidden Israel and their king, who was no longer in touch with God. His methods were totally successful for almost six weeks, with Israel's whole army spellbound like a mouse before a snake.

It is extraordinary to consider that this massive, undefeated warrior was killed by a teenage boy who wore no armour, carried no shield or sword and used only the sling of a shepherd. This is God's power, as He used the ordinary to smash the great. Here is the invincible crushed by the seemingly vulnerable.

---

5   Renner, Rick, Dressed to Kill.

MIND BATTLE

When the giants stood against me in the late 1980s, the onslaught against my mind was incessant.

During this time, my thoughts and imaginations became clouded and distorted. My emotions seemed to be on some huge roller coaster ride. Cynicism, self pity and wrong attitudes tried to invade my thinking. Distrust and distorted thoughts sought to push me aside into my own exile. Even my thoughts toward God, His promises and His faithfulness became twisted. I had to take my thoughts prisoner. Then I made a major discovery. Despite their massive size, giants manoeuvrer best on a 0.2 m (8inch) battlefield. That battlefield is the space between our ears - the mind.

I had never known an assault in my thought life that could compare with what I was experiencing. My whole mind seemed to be buffeted with a cloud of despair and negativity. Satan is the master of mind games. Rick Renner puts it this way:

> **"The Devil loves to make a playground out of peoples' minds. He delights in filling their emotions and senses with illusions that captivate their minds and ultimately destroy them."**

I struggled with an incessant bombardment that seemed to magnify greatly in the night hours. The thoughts of defeat, failure, confusion, doubt and torment were so forceful that they would wake me out of the deepest sleep. I began to search the Scriptures for answers. One Scripture became the key.

> *"For though we walk (live) in the flesh, we are not carrying on our warfare according to the flesh and using mere human weapons. (For the weapons of our warfare are not physical [weapons of flesh and blood], but they are mighty before God for the overthrow and destruction of strongholds,*

[Inasmuch as we] refute arguments and theories and reasonings and every proud and lofty thing that sets itself up against the [true] knowledge of God; and we lead every thought and purpose away captive into the obedience of Christ (the Messiah, the Anointed One),"
2 Corinthians 10:3-5, Amplified Bible

This scripture clarified my situation and may for the ones you face. Firstly, we read here of our warfare that is not carnal or natural. We read of strongholds or fortresses built against us. Amazingly, these strongholds are all summarised in the realm of thoughts, reasonings and elevated things that raise themselves up forcibly against the knowledge of God. This certainly portrays the clear role of the giants we face and the thing that we must do to counteract and turn about the mental assault. I began to study this scripture and found great keys in verse 5. Here is my paraphrasing;

"We are casting down (demolishing with violence, destroying) imaginations (reasonings and thoughts) and <u>every</u> high thing (elevated, barrier) that exalts itself (raises itself, lifts itself) against the knowledge of God".

Like a massive demolition ball, God has supernaturally anointed us and gifted us to utterly smash the giant mind assaults from Hell. Not only does God tell us that we are equipped to smash down Satan's mental devices but we are to make captive every thought "to the obedience of Christ".[6]

When giants stand against us, we have to forcefully seize our thoughts, taking them prisoner. The giant killer must bring every thought into subjection. We must, by a calculated decision, arrest speculation, reasoning and imagining. The way we think becomes a choice.

---

6   II Corinthians 10:5

"For as he thinketh in his heart, so is he" Proverbs 23:7

It is significant that the word "thinks" is well translated, "to act as gatekeeper".[7] We must guard our minds as a gatekeeper controlling what we allow to enter.

Our thoughts, when left unchecked, begin to control our emotions and our emotions then impact our whole body, stripping our strength, reducing our endurance and targeting our will to succeed, continue and prevail.

Israel had succumbed to the mind games of Goliath but David came with his mind set like a steel strap.

His mind was not filled with failure nor did his emotions cause him to hang his head. This giant Goliath had brought David to his day of destiny.

David will always be remembered for his defeat of Goliath. What will we be remembered for?

"SEEK THE DECISIVE BATTLE. WHAT GOOD DOES IT DO US TO WIN TEN SCRAPS OF NO CONSEQUENCE IF WE LOSE THE ONE THAT COUNTS? I WANT TO FIGHT BATTLES THAT DECIDE THE FATE OF EMPIRES."[8]

At one stage of my ministry, I was challenged to step out of my comfort zone into a large, but less certain, place that would stretch me massively. A friend spoke to me and said these words:

"Why play with marbles when you can roll boulders?"

We can battle with board members over the ply of toilet paper or the colour of a wall to be painted. I want to be part of major God-directed campaigns that will touch nations and perhaps it is the same for you.

---

7   Strong's H8176
8   The Virtues of War, (A novel of Alexander the Great), page 177.

King David's extraordinary life was one of mighty triumphs and tragic failures, yet he will always be remembered chiefly for his great, empire-framing, epic defeat of the undefeated Philistine champion Goliath of Gath. The graphic image of David holding the severed head of Israel's tormentor has been the subject of vast numbers of artists and the symbol of hope to multitudes of people facing seemingly insurmountable odds.

As the sandalled foot of the teenage shepherd stepped up onto the chain-mailed body of the prostrate giant Goliath, the roars and bellowed shouts of the Israeli army must have filled the air like thunder.

As David stooped down to pull the huge sword from his victim's scabbard, the roar of triumph would have intensified until the moment when its honed edge severed its owner's head. Then a frenzy of unbridled emotions and triumph would have sent the whole Israel army headlong after the now terrified Philistine host.

In the space of a few seconds, the destiny of a whole nation had eternally changed.

It is difficult to imagine any event in Israel's history as significant as this extraordinary victory. As Goliath's massive body crashed to the earth, history changed. A triumphant warrior rose up, who took his nation into an amazing time of prosperity, strength and worship. He set a course for the coming of the Messiah.

History has revealed many moments that have seen global change. On 11 September 2001, I sat with my wife Jacque and watched the terrorist destruction of the World Trade Centre and realized that this event had changed our world forever.

In the words of Alexander the Great, we need to win conflicts, "that decide the fate of empires". We need to understand that each giant we defeat has history-shaping impact.

Let us not involve ourselves in meaningless argumentative scraps or foolish battles of wills but rather let us see the huge picture and opportunity placed before us and move out with large dreams onto the great arena of faith.

We have huge battles to win and powerful giants to defeat. Significant decisive battles lie ahead that will totally transform nations.

GIANTS SLAIN BRING GREAT REWARD

"And David spake to the men that stood by him, saying, What shall be done to the man that killeth this Philistine, and taketh away the reproach from Israel? for who is this uncircumcised Philistine, that he should defy the armies of the living God?" 1 Samuel 17:26

David's attitude towards Goliath is so refreshing. He doesn't refer to him as a giant but simply another Philistine. He doesn't see the size of the Philistine but is sickened by the reproach being levelled against his nation. The Hebrew word translated "reproach" is cherpah[9] and means "to be scorned, despised, reproached and put in contempt".

Not only does David refer to the giant simply as "this Philistine" but reminds the men of Israel's army that he is an uncircumcised man alienated from the God of Israel, unable to draw on the great resources of the Lord of Hosts, and in fact God's enemy.

"Who is he?" asks David, "What is so special about him that he can step out in defiance of the army of the God who is alive, active and the all powerful controller of the Universe?"

"Surely," thinks David, "There must be a reward for killing him." Something in David refuses to consider the ferocity, size or intimidation of the giant. He only sees the need for this reproach to cease and reward to be given.

For David, the reward offered was great wealth, marriage to a beautiful woman of great standing and influence and tax exemption for his family. This was King Saul's reward. God's reward went far beyond. The ultimate gain from Goliath's death was the chance to grasp kingship over Israel, wealth and power beyond understanding and the wonderful privilege of, not only to be part of the line of Messiah, but to play a significant part in ushering in the ultimate Kingdom.

Goliath was a gift from God to David wrapped in 91 kg (200 pounds) of chain mail armour and carrying a spear with a 9 kg (20 pound) head. Fearsome and intimidating, but nevertheless God's gift.

9   Strong's H2761

Every giant that you and I confront is potential laden. It is a stepping stone to a new place of opportunity with God. That giant is a door to new possibilities and opportunities.

My friend, that giant that confronts you, leering, intimidating and emotionally immobilizing, needs to be seen through eyes like David. In fact, through your eyes it must be seen as your stepping stone – a great opportunity to step into a new place of authority, responsibility, wealth, influence and Kingdom impact.

David realized that a great God-given opportunity had presented itself in a remarkable way. He must have been acutely aware that this was his strategic opportunity.

When the giants of life begin to roar in our faces with menace and threat we have to ask the same question that David asked:

"What is the reward for killing this great opponent?"

GOD ALWAYS HAS HIS MAN

"And he (Goliath) stood and cried unto the armies of Israel, and said unto them, why are ye come to set your battle in array? am not I a Philistine, and ye servants to Saul? choose you a man for you, and let him come down to me. If he be able to fight with me, and to kill me, then will we be your servants: but if I prevail against him, and kill him, then shall ye be our servants, and serve us. And the Philistine said, I defy the armies of Israel this day; give me a man, that we may fight together."
1 Samuel 17:8-10

Goliath's intimidation seemed unending. King Saul scratched his head and sat in a bewildered state. Israel's army were already mentally defeated and the situation looked hopeless. Israel's army seemed ready to be totally overrun when God revealed His plan. "Send me out a man!" had been Goliath's bellowing threat. Seventy nine times he had cried out without response but, now on the eightieth shout, God's man was ready.

King Saul and his frightened army cringed at the defiant taunts of the Philistine champion Goliath. His words thundered across the field as if rising directly from the cavernous regions of the underworld. At each utterance from the giant's mouth, the bewildered army froze a little more.

"Give me a man that we might fight together!" roared this "unstoppable" champion. The only response was silence and cold sweat.

How often in the dark night hours have you been awakened by the roars of defiance that attack your worth, your capacity to fulfil your destiny, or the future of your family? How often have you heard the roars of doubt-filled words that probe the most vulnerable regions of your mind and soul?

These shouts and roars draw out the David in you and me onto the field of conflict. We either shrink back or rise up on the inside knowing that we are not the giant's prey but that he is ours.

God always has his man or woman for the task. In every age it seems the giants cry out, "Send me out a man!" The giant Goliath had been shouting his defiant roar for 40 long days as the army of Israel shuddered in feat but God had prepared His man. In the lonely hills of Bethlehem, God had been honing and preparing His man for this critical moment in Israel's history. All over the world the same shout, "Give me a man that we might fight together!" is resonating and God has been preparing those who will come onto the field to confront them.

The roars will either paralyse with despair or cause the David within you to step out onto the field. "Give me a man!" The words resonated through the spirit realm. Some people cringe in terror, while others stand up on the inside with holy determination and resolve.

PREPARATION OF GIANT KILLERS

"Numerous armies of raw and undisciplined troops are but masses of men dragged to slaughter."
Vegetius, Roman Historian 380 A.P.[10]

---

10   Living in the Combat Zone, Rick Renner pg 133

The sign at Scott Airbase, Illinois, makes a powerful statement "An untrained soldier is just a target".[11] As we sat in our armchairs watching the Gulf War and then Operation Desert Storm, the technological superiority of the United States and Coalition Forces made the Iraqi Army simply look like targets.

As the Allied Forces surrounded Berlin in World War II, the Nazi forces were in chaos. The Russian forces were hardened warriors whose hatred of the Third Reich was white hot. They had seen the death of millions of their countrymen, both military and civilian, at the hand of the Nazi war machine. They ruthlessly ravaged and crushed their enemy. The American and British forces, with memories of the Blitz on London, their massive losses at D-Day and months of bitter fighting through hedgerows and hamlets, also came to bring the death blow.

With huge depletion of Hitler's forces, young German boys as young as 12-years-old were put in uniform, given a rifle and sent into the streets of Berlin to face ruthless, skilled veterans.

The blood of these young untrained boys ran like rivers through the streets of the decimated capital. A merciless Soviet force sliced through these boys and old men like a knife through butter.

God does not send untrained boys as lambs to the slaughter. He hones his warriors and prepares them to stand strong in the day of battle.

Certainly, David was only a teenager but he was God's highly trained warrior. David himself declared:

> *"He teacheth my hands to war; so that a bow of steel is broken by mine arms."* 2 Samuel 22:35

> *"Blessed be the LORD my strength, which teacheth my hands to war, and my fingers to fight: My goodness, and my fortress; my high tower, and my deliverer; my shield, and he in whom I trust; who subdueth my people under me."* Psalm 144:1-2

---

11   McHenry's Quips, Quotes Other Notes 800, page 237

Alone in the desolate, windswept, lonely hills near Bethlehem, God had a young freckle-faced youth for kingly dominion. He had put upon him the anointing of an invincible leader and warrior.

God prepared David as his man of courage and responsibility. Lions and bears roamed these lonely hills, which made nights here particularly terrifying for the shepherd boys. The roars and growls of hungry predators must have sent shivers of terror up their spines. Perhaps the glint of a lion's eyes as it crouched and circled the flock or the grunting of a bear in the near vicinity would send paralysing shock and fear through their hearts

In 1974, I spent four months crossing central Africa from East to West. During that time, our team camped in military tents each night. One night stands out vividly in my memory. We were camped in the open bush, near the base of Mount Kilimanjaro. I was standing by the fire on guard in the early morning hours. I can still recall the roar of lions, shattering the stillness of the cold night air.

The lions seemed so close. The sound of their roaring seemed to resonate through my being. I immediately threw a pile of wood on the fire to discourage these awesome carnivores.

In this isolated, desolate place, David learned the power of the high praises of God. He learned authority in the spirit and skill with his weaponry. Young David learned to worship God on those lonely nights. As he played his shepherd's harp and militantly worshipped God, he drove away the spirits of fear that tried to take hold of his mind and emotions.

At night, his praise and worship made him a master in the realm of the spirit. This young, already anointed warrior king, in the cold chill of the Bethlehem nights, worshipped and praised his way into a place of dominion and authority. Every devil of fear and torment fled from him and those shepherds with him. In these cold lonely nights, with the haunting whistle of the wind and the strange sounds of the unseen stalking terrors of the night, the "psalmist of Israel" became a master in the spiritual realm.

"Let the high praises of God be in their mouth, and a twoedged sword in their hand; To execute vengeance upon the heathen, and punishments upon the people; To bind their kings with chains, and their nobles with fetters of iron;" Psalm 149:6-8

The Lion of the tribe of Judah, hundreds of years before his birth in a stable nearby, began to roar out of the mind, soul and spirit of David. So powerful grew David's reputation as a militant worshipper, whose psalms and worship drove Hell away, that he was summoned to use his honed gift to drive off the tormenting demons that sought to derange King Saul of Israel.

God had broken through in his inner man, to a place of supernatural and indomitable confidence and certainty in Him.

Here he learned that the high praises of God have the power to bind up authorities and powers and cause the natural realm to submit to divine authority.

Goliath's demise was prepared in this place of total obscurity, loneliness and even rejection. The certainty and confidence required for the great future encounter was established in these chilly nights.

By day, David took the time to practise with the weapons of a shepherd. He knew that God was training his fingers and hands for natural battle. By night, he was growing in courage and spiritual authority through the power of praise.

"Judah, (praise) thou art he whom thy brethren shall praise: thy hand shall be in the neck of thine enemies... Judah (praise) is a lion's whelp: from the prey, my son, thou art gone up: he stooped down, he couched as a lion, and as an old lion; who shall rouse him up? The sceptre shall not depart from Judah (praise)..." Genesis 49:8-10

God has made it abundantly clear to us 21st Century giant killers that the high praises of God still wield great dominion in the dimension of the spirit and that the praising man or woman will keep their foot on the giant's neck. The strong sceptre of dominion is truly in their hands.[12]

Word of David's spiritual authority and trained hands for war reached the ears of King Saul, whose servants sought him out to drive the tormenting spirits from Saul's life. They sought for a man who was cunning, who played on a harp, whose worship would have dominion over the demons that buffeted Saul and to bring healing.[13]

The response to this search tells us much about David and God's preparation of "His man".

> *"Then answered one of the servants, and said, Behold, I have seen a son of Jesse the Bethlehemite, that is cunning in playing, and a mighty valiant man, and a man of war, and prudent in matters, and a comely person, and the LORD is with him."* 1 Samuel 16:18

How had he gained this reputation? His own family had not seen it. His own family treated him poorly. His own father failed to even acknowledge his existence to Samuel, and did so only as an afterthought.[14]

Most people saw him as a mere youth yet those who really knew him described him as a mighty valiant man and a man of war.

The giant killer was ready. His training was complete. He walked from these lonely hills into his place of destiny as Israel's beloved warrior king.

Perhaps you are currently in a chilly place of loneliness or rejection where the sounds in your ears are those of beasts of Hell plotting your demise. Perhaps in the night hours you are assaulted in your mind by roars of failure, growls of unrest and threats of destruction.

You are in a great place to learn the power of the high praises of God and to allow God to train you in the use of His weaponry.

Like David, lonely hills and desolate Australian outback are the

12   Psalms 110
13   I Samuel 16:16
14   I Samuel 16:11

places where I love to pray and seek God.

There is a unique smell that permeates the air of the Flinders Ranges in South Australia. It is a strange mix of the foliage in this area, gums and native pines, with the scent of thousands of kangaroos that inhabit this place. Rugged ramparts, which glow golden and red in the afternoon light streaming through the dust laden air, seem to rise as great sentinels of God's grandeur. As I breathe deeply and gaze at the stoic ramparts of Rawnsley's Bluff and the long southern wall of Wilpena Pound, I am engulfed with an awareness of God's power pulsing through my body. As a 15-year-old boy several decades ago, I had been awakened from a deep sleep as we camped in this rugged beautiful jewel of the sun-drenched land of Australia that I love so dearly. Here I experienced something that would change me spiritually forever. It was a beautiful starry night, with the sky a great canopy of stars, as dozens of young men on a National Fitness Camp climbed exhausted into our sleeping bags after a day of intense hiking and climbing.

In the early hours of the morning, I woke abruptly and looked up to see a very large male figure, white in appearance, standing over me. One of my friends awoke and saw what I know to have been an Angel of God. I was awestruck. Something happened that I could not explain. It was an encounter with God so powerful that, for the past four decades, I have been drawn to fast and pray and passionately seek the face of God in this area.

Here, God has met me and visited me in seasons when my craving for God has been powerfully intense.

Here, I have been able to identify with David as he cried:

"O God, thou art my God; early will I seek thee: my soul thirsteth for thee, my flesh longeth for thee in a dry and thirsty land, where no water is; To see thy power and thy glory, so as I have seen thee in the sanctuary." Psalm 63:1-2

What can compare with those awesome encounters when we are alone with Him in a desolate place, far from the clamour of daily life, phone and appointments and so much of the "wood, hay and stubble" of so-called "ministry"? Here, the tangible, soul-shaking, overwhelming presence of the weight of His glory comes flooding as a torrent into my thirsting soul. Here I can feel with David as he writes:

> *"I will lift up mine eyes unto the hills, from whence cometh my help."* Psalm 121:1

Here, I sense something of the encounter of Moses on Mount Sinai. Here, my whole being pulses with the same pulse of God that Elijah felt in the lonely windswept hills of Tishbe in Gilead. It was from a desolate place like this that God commanded Elijah to go to King Ahab with eternal authority and declare:

> *"...As the Lord God of Israel liveth, before whom I stand..."* 1 Kings 17:1

In the loneliness of the Bethlehem hills David was shaped, honed and prepared as God's sharp threshing instrument.

Alone in the Australian outback, I experience a frightening awareness of hostile powers and principalities. Confronting these and standing resolute causes a defiant sense of holy confidence and authority to rise within.

We are often so busy with meetings, deadlines, programs, financial pressures, locked in with the demands and bleating of the flocks, that we fail to draw aside (for weeks if necessary) to hone the blunt edge of our axe.

> *"If the iron be blunt, and he do not whet the edge, then must he put to more strength: but wisdom is profitable to direct."* Ecclesiastes 10:10

Alone with God, in intense prayer and fasting, we experience a great honing of our spiritual edge.

Several years ago, I set aside a number of days to go to the Flinders

Ranges where I had often gone alone for weeks at a time to passionately seek intimacy with God.

In this place I had experienced His power more significantly than at any other place. The encounters with God in this red dust paradise of rocks and gums built and shaped my walk with the Lord.

It was a dark night as I walked onto a hill that looked upon the blue-grey ramparts that rose as a massive sentinel before me. My knees buckled as the intense billows of God surged through me. God's awesome power caused my whole being to tremble. Then I began to hear the voice of God within me.

> "...I remember thee, the kindness of thy youth, the love
> of thine espousals, when thou wentest after me in the
> wilderness, in a land that was not sown."
> Jeremiah 2:2

I could sense the cry of God's heart. Where have you been? Why don't you crave for me with the same intensity and desperation that drove you as a young man? Where is that ferocious passion, that unbridled zeal that drew you alone with me for weeks at a time when all you wanted in life was me?

I felt God really drive home His feelings. I had been very busy in the months leading up to this time and my prayer life had greatly suffered. I was not passionately hungering for God with the intensity that had driven me years before. Now, God spoke to me as clearly as I've ever heard.

"Tim, do you think I am honouring you for your current spiritual state? No. I am honouring a young man who came out here to lay hold of Me with all that was in him. Tell Me have you seen him recently?"

I sobbed, knowing that all God wanted from me was a passionate desire to know Him intimately and to walk with Him.

God must have loved walking with Adam in the "cool of the day".[15] God had chosen the lonely hills surrounding Bethlehem, a place of isolation and wild beasts, to train his great giant killer. He would not walk into his great moment in history as an untrained warrior.

---

15   Genesis 3:8

It was in the desolate, foreboding desert of Judea that God forged His messenger of power, John the Baptist. It was in the desolate loneliness of the Judean hills that the ultimate giant killer, the great destroyer of death and hell, full of the Holy Ghost, endured 40 days and nights of trial and temptation. It was out of this lonely desolate place, that Jesus emerged in the power of the Spirit, ready to once and for all, strip the satanic giant of the ages of all his power.

In hundreds of hours alone with God, he was supernaturally trained by God to worship, to take hold of his Great Shepherd and to ply with mighty confidence weapons of warfare.

My friend, it is in the secret place of the Most High, that you will be trained for war. It is alone with God, in that secret place, fasting and seeking His face, that God will train you in the application and use of the spiritual manifestations of power, demonstration and knowledge, so lacking in the body of Christ today. It is in the long, desperate searching and passion for His word, hours spent dissecting, inquiring and devouring that God will hone in us a sharp two-edged sword of massive influence.

Jesus regularly withdrew from daily ministry and go into the wilderness or onto a mountain to commune with the Father. On occasions He took His disciples. This was an established habit in His ministry. Today, the need of the Church is for its leaders to take time away with God. Ministers should set times in their calendars when they pull aside with God, for weeks if necessary, to sharpen their spiritual gifts, to tune their spiritual ears and to crave after God's mighty presence and power.

David had been prepared and trained as God's warrior. He was recognised by his peers as "a mighty and valiant man of war" before he had even stepped onto the field of human conflict.

In the perilous, unchartered waters into which the 21st Century Church is embarking, God needs His men and women to be prepared warriors with David's qualifications. His resume in I Samuel 16:17 reads:

1. He was a mighty valiant man.
2. He was a man of war.
3. He was prudent in matters.
4. He was a comely (approachable, down to earth) person.
5. The Lord was with him.

These were his qualifications not after his victory over Goliath. They were the qualifications and reputation he had gained while he was still a shepherd boy in the hills around Bethlehem.

David had been thoroughly trained for his moment of triumph over Goliath. He had finished his apprenticeship with honours. He was ready.

How is our preparation proceeding for our greatest days of opportunity?

Are our skills being honed, the gifts of God in our life practised? Is the Word of God become the deadly sword in our mouth? Our greatest days of triumph and massive victories are approaching so rapidly. Let us be totally prepared for God's moments.

"THE CHINESE USE TWO BRUSH STROKES TO WRITE THE WORD "CRISIS".
ONE BRUSH STROKE STANDS FOR DANGER;
THE OTHER FOR OPPORTUNITY.
IN A CRISIS, BE AWARE OF THE DANGER –
BUT RECOGNISE THE OPPORTUNITY."[16]

危机

---

16   John F. Kennedy (1917-1963), Speech in Indianapolis, April, 1959.

GIANT KILLERS SEIZE THEIR DAY OF OPPORTUNITY

When John F. Kennedy declared, in his Indianapolous speech of 1959, the meanings of these Chinese symbols for crisis, he was certainly outlining David's position: grave danger mingled with huge opportunity.

David truly seized his opportunity. He gripped it firmly with both hands and stepped into his destiny.

David was not the only person in the ranks that day whose skill could have brought down the giant. In Judges 20:16 we read:

> *"Among all this people there were seven hundred chosen men lefthanded; every one could sling stones at a hair breadth, and not miss."*

We read of many slingers of the tribe of Benjamin who could deliver a stone with such accuracy that they could strike to within a hair's breadth and never miss. Any of these slingers could have slain Goliath but they did not take the field. David took the field and seized his great opportunity. Many men and women carry gifts of God, can preach powerfully, teach with confidence, and even operate in the supernatural gifting of God but through timidity, apathy or other involvements in life, they never take the field. Many people will look back in old age and be full of remorse because they failed to put themselves out onto the field of conflict. David declared and spoke destiny. Then he placed himself in a position where God could take him into his place in the eternal arena of faith.

We cannot let the roar of the giant's intimidation, nor the giant of our own insecurity, prevent us from taking the field with bold tenacity and ferocious intent.

Almost everyone has heard of Levi Strauss or has worn the jeans. Levi took his opportunity. Opportunity seldom knocks twice, so Levi Strauss opened the door after the first knock. Like many other men,

Strauss went to California with hopes of making his fortune there. He did make a fortune but not the way he had planned. He set out with a load of heavy canvas fabric, from which he planned to sell sections for tents and wagon covers. Upon his arrival, the first miner who saw his product said, "You should have brought pants". The seasoned miner further explained how there weren't any pants strong enough to endure the arduous conditions of mining. Levi Strauss immediately made the miner a pair of work pants and struck gold. Opportunity only becomes opportunity when we embrace it as such.[17]

> **"The reason why so many people never get anywhere in life is because when opportunity knocks, they are out in the backyard looking for four leaf clovers."[18]**

> **"…If you have spent most of your waking time thinking about your mission, when the opportunity comes your way, you will grasp it with such vigour that it will cry for mercy."[19]**

> **"While we stop to think, we often miss our opportunity."[20]**

Small opportunities are often the beginning of great opportunities.

> **"The opportunity of a lifetime must be seized during the lifetime of the opportunity."[21]**

In 1975, I was pioneering my first church. I was a school teacher in a country town and had been saved for only one year. I had committed myself to hours of prayer per day and at least ten days fasting per month. God opened my heart to step out and pioneer a church.

17   McHenry's Quips, Quotes, Other Notes, page 176
18   Walter Chrysler page 585
19   Shaka Zulu (Africa's Alexander the Great), page 23
20   Publius Syrus (100BC), Maxima
21   Unknown

People began to gather to us, a building was renovated and purchased and God began to open exciting doors.

A friend came to me from our mother church. He knew much more of God's word than I and for years had been faithfully serving the church. He was somewhat annoyed with me and asked, "I have served God for years and you a short time, so why is God using you this way and not me?"

I was taken aback and somewhat confused. I realised that it was simply because I had seized my opportunity. David did not wait for someone else to seize the opportunity with Goliath. He sensed his destiny and seized it with both hands.

Opportunities from the Lord will present themselves to us regularly. Perhaps others can do the job as well as we. But, like David, let us boldly step onto the field and grasp our God-given destiny with both hands. Even as you read these words the greatest opportunity of your life may be knocking at your door. Step out of the ranks with courage and resolve. This is your day.

GIANT KILLERS TAKE THE FIELD

The S.A.S. (Special Air Services) of the British Army is a proudly elite force that is respected all over the world. Their famous motto is: "Who dares wins". In Australia, we have a number of expressions that relate to being ready to move speedily into action. "First in best dressed", is a comical but expressive challenge to be the first to take the field. David laid hold of his opportunity and took the field. Nothing ever seems to occur until we step out with a proactive attitude. Gilbert and Sullivan had this in mind in their musical 'Iolanthe' when the peers sang, "Nothing ventured, nothing win".

Often, circumstances may seem totally unsuitable for us to step out. The courageous individual steps out even when it seems impossible. Jonathan (son of Saul), accompanied by his armour bearer, stepped out to confront the whole Philistine garrison with one sword (1 Samuel 14: 6-23). David's mighty men crossed the Jordan in full flood to put to flight the enemies in the valley (1 Chronicles 11:15).

It is said that Beethoven, perhaps the greatest composer of all, came to a crisis point in his life. His hearing was gone completely and his fingers had thickened, making them useless to play music. A friend heard him pounding the piano keys and shouting,

"I will seize my destiny by the throat."

With these major disabilities, he both wrote and conducted his famous Ninth Symphony. Despite every setback, he grasped his destiny with both hands and wrote one of the most famous pieces of music ever penned.

Let us never allow fear, timidity or the face of giants to prevent us boldly and decisively seizing the opportunities God presents us with.

This was David's day, which he had been born, trained and prepared for. The opposition was massive, taunting, menacing and capable of crushing him with a single blow but in the words of John Mason,

"THE DOOR OF OPPORTUNITY SWINGS ON THE HINGES OF OPPOSITION."

God had a man - a freckle-faced teenage shepherd boy of ruddy complexion, looking after a few sheep in the rugged lion infested hills around Bethlehem. He was "the least" of his father's sons but a warrior in training on the lonely Judean hills.

David will always be known as the giant killer of the ages. The picture of the young shepherd boy, without armour, confronting the terrifying champion of Philistia echoes through Eternity. The conjured picture of the ruddy faced teenager, eyes ablaze with God's fire, rushing against a 3 m (10 foot) tall undefeated warrior armoured with heavy mail and carrying brutal weaponry, inspires and thrills.

The impact of this seemingly one-sided battle has not only inspired multitudes to be unafraid of whatever the enemy can bring against them and to realize that, "if God be for them, who or what can be against them". The victory ushered in a whole new kingdom and prepared a throne of dominion that ushered the line of Messiah.

The giant you kill is your stepping stone to a new place of authority, provision, dominion and boldness in God. The giant that you bring down is a great stepping stone to a new day for you, your family, your church and even the nations of the Earth.

After David's time, the Bible and history no longer reveal giants on the Earth. In David's final battle over the four giants of Gath, it seems that these races of extraordinary huge beings ceased.

God is always searching for his man (or woman) to seize his opportunity and take the field.

David, like Caleb, had an extraordinary spirit.

"What is the reward for killing this great opponent?"

DAVID

GIANT KILLERS ARE OFTEN MISUNDERSTOOD AND SLANDERED

"And Eliab his eldest brother heard when he spake unto the men; and Eliab's anger was kindled against David, and he said, Why camest thou down hither? and with whom hast thou left those few sheep in the wilderness? I know thy pride, and the naughtiness of thine heart; for thou art come down that thou mightest see the battle. And David said, What have I now done? Is there not a cause?" 1 Samuel 17:28-29

The nostrils of David's eldest brother Eliab flared with hostility and wrath at David's words. Go back to "those few sheep in the wilderness".[1] In front of the men, Eliab, while personally afraid to challenge Goliath, endeavoured to belittle David and question his qualifications for battle. You only have a "few sheep" out there in an insignificant wilderness place.

Slander, ridicule and opposition often come from those closest to them. This seems to be a common denominator for giant killers.

Eliab certainly aimed to bring David down to his level of fear and inactivity. When a bunch of crabs are placed in a bucket, those trying to escape over the sides will be pulled back by those below.

Eliab set out to totally belittle David. He questioned why David was even there, and let him know that he had no place among the warriors.

"Why camest thou down hither?"²

Eliab continued to question and accuse David before men of the army.

> *"...with whom hast thou left those few sheep in the wilderness?"³*

> *"...I know the pride and the naughtiness of thine heart..."⁴*

Eliab declared his brother to be a naughty, arrogant boy, full of pride and who presumed to have more authority than was warranted. Before the soldiers, he reminded David that he was a mere insignificant shepherd boy with just a few sheep in a remote wilderness place. Effectively, he declared to David, "You are out of your depth. You don't belong here. You are a nobody."

This is precisely what Satan tells us. He informs us that we have no right to step out and attempt great things. He tells us that what we do is of no significance and points to the scale of the work we do.

How often are men and women of God judged by the size of the church they pastor? They are made to seem of no importance because they minister in a remote place out of the public eye. I listened intently as the great American statesman preacher T.D. Jakes talked of the years pastoring a seemingly small, insignificant church in West Virginia. Asked when he began preaching the great sermons we hear today, he explained that he had been preaching them over many years in obscurity in West Virginia. Today, he thrills and inspires multitudes with the impacting, power-filled revelation that flows like liquid fire from his mouth. It is inspiring to know that for many years this man of God was ministering his mighty messages, alive with revelation, to a <u>few hundred peop</u>le.

2   I Samuel 17:28
3   I Samuel 17:28
4   I Samuel 17:28

David certainly was a shepherd to a small flock in an obscure wilderness place. But it was here that God had trained him for this moment. Like Elijah walking out of the remote regions of Tishbe in Gilead into the king's palace and onto the pages of history, David walks out of the lonely hills around Bethlehem onto the stage of global history. We are certainly instructed not to despise the day of small beginnings.

Eliab's next line of attack is focussed on David's character: the "naughtiness", meaning "wretchedness, deformity and negative attitude"[5], of David's heart. It is strange that God called him, "a man after his own heart".[6] Giant killers do not allow people to arrogantly stand and judge the intentions of their hearts. They know who they are, and whose they are, standing in obedience to fulfil their God-ordained purposes.

Eliab even cast doubt on David's integrity by asking him with whom he had irresponsibly left "those few sheep". The sarcastic, acidic tongue of his brother aimed to stifle his resolve and bring him back to the stature of the intimidated army. But David could not be swayed.

Eliab had attacked David's lack of qualification for battle and had questioned his character and responsibility, declaring him to be proud and wretched of heart and considered him no more than a naughty young stickybeak, an unqualified "rubber-necker".

What things have been said about you and me? How often have we moved into a place ready to take serious ground in God, only to be assaulted by slander, accusations and lies, often by people of whom we expect much more?

Any man or woman wishing to make an impact for God must be prepared for a tirade of slander and snide acidic accusations aimed to shake and undermine his faith. Noah had to endure incessant abuse and mockery for a century. He must have been glad he had endured when the rain poured down.

David questions, "What have I now done?" (1 Samuel 17:29). This must have been commonplace at home. What had David done this

---

5   Strong's H7455
6   1 Samuel 13:14

time? David must have faced constant accusation and wearing character assassination from his own family. With his eyes aflame like a lion, his face filled with steely resolve, he turned to the soldiers one by one and, like a military commander, shouts: "Is there not a cause?" (1 Samuel 17:29). Giant killers have to stand strong through verbal assault, lies and character assassination and keep the same declaration.

Jealousy shut down the great Welsh revivalist Evan Roberts and closed down numerous great moves of God in the 20th Century.

I have watched the media assault some of our finest Australian ministries, often guided by so-called "well meaning" Christians. So often the attacks come from Christians who spend their time in the "sheep folds listening to the bleating of the flocks".[7]

The front line daring warriors of Christ are generally too passionately motivated to allow Satan to put jealousy in their hearts.

I have found that my hunger and passion to demonstrate the power of God has brought slanderous accusations and especially innuendos against my life and ministry. Often these destructive, unfounded and unchecked rumours hold back opportunities for God's blessing. Praise God that, like David, we can push through everything that the Devil rails against us. Giant killers cannot be stopped.

How did David respond to words that had bombarded him from his older brother Eliab?

When Eliab questioned him, a defiant challenge shot like a dart out of David's mouth. I imagine the stare of illuminated fire filled his eyes as he shouted, "Is there not a cause?" This is not a timid murmur but a warrior's shout of defiance, a shout loud enough to attract all the armed men around him. This was the first challenging, shrill shout they would hear from the young man who would soon be promoted to General of the Army. This would be the first shout of authority from the young man who later inspired the military might of his own elite regiment known as David's mighty men. Immediately, his words rode roughshod over Eliab's cowardly and misinformed remarks.

---

7   Judges 5:16

After David was escorted to King Saul's tent he again faced words of doubt and unbelief. He faces a vote of no confidence.

> *"Thou art not able to go against this Philistine to fight with him: for thou art but a youth, and he a man of war from his youth."* 1 Samuel 17:33

King Saul told him straight out that this was beyond him. He informed him that he is a young untrained youth and that the enemy is not just a man but a proven man of war. But David was not put off, even by the words of his king.

David responds with defiant strength. "This is my resume", he said:

> *"Thy servant kept his father's sheep, and there came a lion, and a bear, and took a lamb out of the flock: And I went out after him, and smote him, and delivered it out of his mouth: and when he arose against me, I caught him by his beard, and smote him, and slew him."*
> 1 Samuel 17:34-36

David had to overcome every verbal outburst from his seniors even from his own family. Are you able to overcome the onslaught of doubt hurled at you from all angles? These are words formed in Hell's forges, calculated and planned to quench your zeal, fill you with doubt and bring into question your ability to fulfil the task. Before facing Goliath, David had to run the gauntlet of doubt filled words. These word onslaughts will always precede your walk onto the arena of faith, where your victory will see you step up into the new place of destiny.

How powerfully negative words ring in the mind, often years after they have been uttered. Maybe you have had words like these directed at you during the course of your life:

"You will never make it."

"You can't do this; leave it to someone who can."

"Who do you think you are to attempt what others couldn't do?"

"You are dumb, stupid, and incapable of achieving anything."

I think David had faced years of doubt from his family. I think this is summed up by his question: "What have I now done?"[8].

In today's language, we would probably ask, "What have I done this time?"

The tirades and verbal assaults that came from Goliath had already paralysed a whole army. How did a teenage boy cope with the insulting roars and threats that gushed like a blanket of barbed terror from the giant's mouth?

When the giant saw David he "disdained" him. He was insulted that he had to fight a mere boy carrying sticks (rod and staff). He mocked him and asked if he was considered a dog to be hunted off with sticks.

His mockery turned to curses then threats of his mangled flesh being fed to the vultures and carrion birds of the air.

Disgust, derision, sarcasm, curses and threats of a horrendous death poured out like a satanic river that aimed to bring David's faith to nought.

When Goliath sought to intimidate the seemingly ill-equipped young man and to emphasise the precarious lowliness of his situation, David responded like this (my paraphrase of 1 Samuel 17:45):

> *"You come in all your military might, your great armour and tremendous sword but I come in the calling, purpose, might and name of the God of the armies of Israel. It is Him who you fight today."*

After he heard all of Goliath's taunts, he declared to the giant his standing and authority with God, which overruled all the negative verbal assault. He clearly outlined that, this is God's assignment and then told Satan what he himself will do. He outlines the "wills" of the day (1 Samuel 17:46):

1. "This day will the LORD deliver thee into mine hand."
2. "I will smite thee, and take thine head from thee."
3. "I will give the carcases of the host of the Philistines this day unto the fowls of the air, and to the wild beasts of the earth."

David's defiant, purpose-filled, uncompromising words echoed and <u>reverberated through</u> the valley and indeed the spirit realm.

8   I Samuel 17:26

We underestimate the power of our words. God wants our words to resonate through valleys where our enemies stand in defiance. Our words, under God's anointing, are so powerful that, like the words of Jesus, they impact every realm.

David the giant killer refused to be in any way turned from God's purpose by his family, his king or the giant himself. He answered every negative word with his own faith-filled, God-inspired, anointed words of triumph. We must do the same.

GIANT KILLERS ENCOURAGE[9]

One of the most difficult things I faced, during my own onslaught from Hell in 1988, was accusation and blame that seemed so unjust, unfeeling and misinformed. I found that so few of our friends seemed to understand or really care. Indifference caused my mind to magnify everything that was happening. It is during these times that the voice of the giant seems to roar in.

During the worst moments of the attack on our home, I found myself becoming isolated and somewhat distrusting even of Christian brothers and sisters. I found that instead of sympathy and understanding, judgement and legalistic attitudes confronted me. Strong and decisive choices had to be made as to what I would really believe.

During the darkest time, two things stood out like beacons. One of my closest boyhood friends drove to Adelaide with his wife. We went to a restaurant together, talked about my situation and then, in the car park, my friend hugged me and sobbed. Words failed him. With tear-filled eyes he simply expressed his care.

That moment of compassion and care seemed to smash into the face of the giants who confronted me. It seemed like David's situation as he confronted the giant Ishbibenob. The young man Abishai came alongside David, strengthened him, then destroyed the giant.

9   1 Samuel 17:47

Strong, compassionate friends who will stand shoulder to shoulder with us when the giants roar are vital. It is also important for us to be that caring compassionate friend to others when their giants come.

When tragedy strikes, people don't need strong lectures on why the circumstances came nor do they need judgement and accusation. These things isolate and harden the heart in an attitude of defence and survival.

Some time ago, I heard a preacher talk of the American Bald Eagle. At a certain season, this great bird has to shed and replace its feathers. He plucks out his feathers then sits and waits for the replacements to grow. The preacher had asked an old American Indian how the bird survived while it was unable to hunt. The old Indian explained that Bald Eagles that had been through the same process dropped meat to the suffering bird.

Christians who have confronted the savage giants of life are usually the ones who bring the meat of compassion to suffering brothers and sisters.

When the wife of my friend tragically died, I caught the first plane to his city where I spent four days standing with him in his pain. Like the Bald Eagle, I was able to bring him the meat of compassion.

Compassion and genuine concern roar back into the giant's face.

The other incident that stands out like a beacon when I remember that dark time occurred in the home of a great friend we called "The Colonel". He was a Vietnam veteran whom I had led to Christ some years before. He loved to talk of the military and had a huge passion for the nations. As I sat talking with him one morning he leant towards me and simply but strongly declared, "You will come through this because you've got God and you've got guts." He repeated this like the old sergeant on the parade ground. His forceful militant, yet deeply sensitive, words caused a rising up within me. Someone believed in me and spoke words that found the strong man within me and caused him to stand up.

He explained that the fight for the family we were fighting was a more torrid battle than normal combat. He handed me his combat medal from Vietnam.

Another friend, who had seen action in the British Forces (Para-Regiment), heard what the Colonel had done and also pushed a combat medal into my hand.

Their words rang prophetically in my mind as the words of God. God may have used slightly different wording but the intention of purpose was profound to me and very clear.

Some years later, I was ministering in Bendigo, Victoria, Australia. A young man came up to me devastated. His father had left them only weeks before and his heart was broken. A great giant of betrayal and discouragement raged against him.

I took a combat medal from my pocket, looked him in the eye as I pushed the medal into his hand and declared:

> **"You will make it through this because you've got God and you've got guts."**

His eyes lit up and the warrior rose up within him. He has since made it through, been to Bible College and, last I heard, is in youth ministry. A year or so later a young boy in Bendigo came up to me with the same medal and told me how he was given the medal and received the same instructions. He since passed it on to an Evangelist from America who tells the story to young, hurting people across the USA and beyond.

Eliab did everything in his power to discourage, accuse and slander his young brother. We must encourage and build up those about us. The power of our words to give life is limitless. Well-placed words of life and encouragement have the power to impact people's destinies and touch whole nations.

> **"You can do it because you've got God and you've got guts."**

As you read this book, perhaps facing major giants that are roaring against you, though I can't push that medal into your hand, I can give you the same words:

"You can do it because you've got God and you've got guts."

"I SWEAR THAT SO SOON AS AGE WILL PERMIT...I WILL USE FIRE AND STEEL TO ARREST THE DESTINY OF ROME."[10]

"And David said, What have I now done? Is there not a cause?" 1 Samuel 17:29

David, like the great giant killers of history, was driven by a cause.

The great Carthaginian general Hannibal Barca is considered by many as a general as influential as Alexander the Great. His feats in battle were extraordinary.

In 218 BC, Hannibal terrorised Rome after crossing the Pyrenees Alps with his army. He smashed cities and legions, taking over half a million Roman lives. Napoleon was asked whom he considered to be the greatest military general of history and declared:

"And this Hannibal the most audacious of all; the most astonishing, perhaps; so bold, so sure, so great in everything; who at 26 conceived what is hardly conceivable, executed what one may truly call the impossible."[11]

Hannibal took the Carthaginian army over the massive, rocky, snow-covered Pyrenees Alps with horses and war elephants, lost about thirty per cent of his force through attrition, and then for 16 years

10   Childhood quote of Hannibal Barca of Carthage-The Scourge of Rome
11   Marcus Garney

terrified Rome. The cause had burned in his heart from boyhood. It was a seething hatred of Rome that had festered from a child. It had been built into him by his father Hamilcar Barca and events of the first Punic War with Rome. As a young boy the cause that drove his life had been forged. He had seen Rome's merciless brutality unleashed on Carthage. He had seen his homeland ravaged and torn and had lived with the constant vengeful words of his father and peers ringing in his ears. As a young boy he had set his cause and his destiny.

> **"I swear that so soon as age will permit...I will use fire and steel to arrest the destiny of Rome."[12]**

The cause that burned from childhood saw him crush Rome's legions and stand ready to walk into the city of Rome.

His decision not to enter and take the great city has been a source of debate through the centuries. His failure to finalise his utter victory over all the legions, by not taking the final step, ultimately saw Carthage smashed and himself driven into exile and his suicide. This is a great lesson to us to finish the assignments that He gives us. Perhaps his impetuous drive to cross the Alps too soon proved to be costly. The extent of his mighty exploits, however, can never be underestimated. Hannibal is a mighty example from history of a man driven by a burning cause. We need to be driven on and compelled by a Kingdom cause.

As we read the Epistles, we become aware of Paul's unwavering response to the eternal cause. In his letter to the Philippians, he writes:

> *"But what things were gain to me, those I counted loss for Christ. Yea doubtless, and I count all things but loss for the excellency of the knowledge of Christ Jesus my Lord: for whom I have suffered the loss of all things, and do count them but dung, that I may win Christ,"* Philippians 3:7-8

---

12   Hannibal Barca

"Brethren, I count not myself to have apprehended: but this one thing I do, forgetting those things which are behind, and reaching forth unto those things which are before, I press toward the mark for the prize of the high calling of God in Christ Jesus." Philippians 3:13-14

Paul makes it clear that he was filled with purpose and a burning goal to know Christ intimately and the mighty power of His resurrection. He had a cause that nothing could stop, a passion to cover the earth with God's glory.

"I therefore so run, not as uncertainly; so fight I, not as one that beateth the air" 1 Corinthians 9:26

Throughout his writings, Paul reveals the purposeful pursuit of his cause.

Jesus makes every man's sense of purpose and cause clear, so the world fades into insignificance:

"...who for the joy that was set before him endured the cross, despising the shame, and is set down at the right hand of the throne of God." Hebrews 12:2

Jesus knew the horrors of inexplicable torture that He would face, yet He was driven by a cause established before the foundation of the earth. We were His cause.

In this world of total chaos, fear and growing uncertainty, we must be people of a burning cause, and, if necessary loving not our lives unto death.

Giant killers are focussed. They are people of a cause, clear in direction, moving purposefully toward the goal. Myles Munroe in his book *In Pursuit of Purpose* describes the significance of cause and purpose:

"Purpose is the master of motivation and the mother of commitment. It is the source of enthusiasm and the

womb of perseverance. **Purpose gives birth to hope and instils the passion to act...without this vision we can only exist. We feel no passion for living neither do we have a reason to wake up in the morning."**

Some years ago, I had the privilege of spending some quality time with Reinhard Bonnke, the great German evangelist. At lunch, I had a probing request: "Pastor Bonnke, I have been in evangelism for around 30 years, I am now in my 50s. Can you share with me a few words of personal motivation for the future?"

I watched the countenance of this anointed gladiator of so many campaigns change. His eyes focussed with an awesome stare. I could almost see the countless multitudes of souls and the massive seas of humanity stretched out before him. It was as though he had stepped out on the platform of a giant campaign. His voice strengthened as he looked me in the eye. "Souls," he barked, "souls," he barked again, "and after that, more souls". I was sitting with a man whose total purpose for breathing, whose total reason for existence on this planet, is the conquest of human souls. In the past ten years some 50,000,000 people have turned their lives to Christ in his campaigns.

Reinhard knows his cause. He lives to see multitudes of humanity swept into the Kingdom of God, not by the hundreds but by the millions. The quest for souls dominates every waking moment of this great man's life.

Until we are driven and consumed with our cause and purpose, we must be content to live out our lives in the tepid waters of mediocrity.

The great Zulu general, Shaka Zulu, is considered the Alexander the Great of Africa. Even today in KwaZulu-Natal a person who shows boldness and courage will be told,

"I see Shaka in you."

Words on purpose are significant:

> **"...if you want to be a leader you must have a sense of mission. If you want to be a leader who builds enduring monuments, you must be consumed by no other interest but your sense of mission. If you stumble across leadership opportunities, but those opportunities are just fortuitous distraction your work will be like dew drops that evaporate at the rise of the sun, but if you have conditioned your mind, if you have spent most of your waking time thinking about your mission, when the opportunity comes your way, you will grasp it with such vigour that it will cry for mercy."[13]**

David was totally aware of the predicament facing his nation and knew that he had been born for this great cause. To know your cause, your reason for existence, is vital for every giant killer.

Our son-in-law, Russell Evans and his wife Samantha have built one of the greatest youth ministries in the world over the past decade. From the night that God supernaturally met with Russell and implanted a great dream, vision and mission into his heart, I have watched as he and Samantha, together in single-minded passion, establish "Planetshakers Conference" across Australia and now into different nations. In Australia alone, a total of over 20,000 young people register for their conferences. Also in the past four years they have established a powerful church with thousands of members in Melbourne, Australia as they passionately and single-mindedly pursue their destiny.

Recently, I was preaching in St Louis, Missouri, USA. I had several days to spare, so I drove down to Memphis Tennessee. I have always been inspired by the great speeches made by Martin Luther King Jr in the early 1960s. Several years previously I stood on the steps of the Lincoln Memorial in Washington D.C. on the spot from which his great speech, "I have a dream", was delivered. Hundreds of thousands of people had come from all over the USA to see human rights changed for

13   Shaka Zulu (Africa's Alexander the Great), page 23

African American people. Now I stood at the Lorraine Motel looking at the spot where an assassin's bullet had cut down a man whose courage and words had changed the mindset of a generation.

The previous night he had courageously preached a passion-laden message in a Baptist church in Memphis. His theme was, "I have seen the Promised Land". I have listened to this historic message many times and marvel and am deeply moved by his steely, passionate, emotional words that were filled with resolve that steeled his people.

> **"...Well, I don't know what will happen now. We've got some difficult days ahead. But it doesn't matter with me now. Because I've been to the mountaintop. And I don't mind. Like anybody, I would like to live a long life. Longevity has its place. But I'm not concerned about that now. I just want to do God's will. And He's allowed me to go up to the mountain. And I've looked over. And I've seen the Promised Land. I may not get there with you. But I want you to know tonight, that we, as a people will get to the Promised Land. And I'm happy, tonight. I'm not worried about anything. I'm not fearing any man. Mine eyes have seen the glory of the coming of the Lord..."[14]**

Anyone who has stood on the steps of Washington's Lincoln Memorial cannot help but sense the moment in August 1963 when Martin Luther King Jr passionately gave the most famous speech of the 20th Century. Although it is 46 years on, the words still ring aloud in the hearts of men and women world-wide. Here is part of his steely speech made to a standing crowd of over 100,000 people:

> **"Let us not wallow in the valley of despair, I say to you today, my friends.**
> **And so even though we face the difficulties of today and tomorrow, I still have a dream. It is a dream deeply**

---

14   Taken from A Testament Of Hope: The Essential Writings of Martin Luther King, Jr., ed. James M. Washington

rooted in the American dream.

I have a dream that one day this nation will rise up and live out the true meaning of its creed: 'We hold these truths to be self-evident, that all men are created equal.'

I have a dream that one day on the red hills of Georgia, the sons of former slaves and the sons of former slave owners will be able to sit down together at the table of brotherhood.

I have a dream that one day even the state of Mississippi, a state sweltering with the heat of injustice, sweltering with the heat of oppression, will be transformed into an oasis of freedom and justice.

I have a dream that my four little children will one day live in a nation where they will not be judged by the colour of their skin but by the content of their character.

I have a dream today!

I have a dream that one day, down in Alabama, with its vicious racists, with its governor having his lips dripping with the words of 'interposition' and 'nullification' -- one day right there in Alabama little black boys and black girls will be able to join hands with little white boys and white girls as sisters and brothers.

I have a dream today!

I have a dream that one day every valley shall be exalted, and every hill and mountain shall be made low, the rough places will be made plain, and the crooked places will be made straight; 'and the glory of the Lord shall be revealed and all flesh shall see it together.'[15]

This is our hope, and this is the faith that I go back to the South with.

With this faith, we will be able to hew out of the

15   Isaiah 40:4-5 (King James Version of the Holy Bible). Quotation marks are excluded from part of this moment in the text because King's rendering of Isaiah 40:4 does not precisely follow the KJV version from which he quotes (e.g., "hill" and "mountain" are reversed in the KJV). King's rendering of Isaiah 40:5, however, is precisely quoted from the KJV.

mountain of despair a stone of hope. With this faith, we will be able to transform the jangling discords of our nation into a beautiful symphony of brotherhood. With this faith, we will be able to work together, to pray together, to struggle together, to go to jail together, to stand up for freedom together, knowing that we will be free one day.

And this will be the day -- this will be the day when all of God's children will be able to sing with new meaning:

My country 'tis of thee, sweet land of liberty, of thee I sing.

Land where my fathers died, land of the Pilgrim's pride, From every mountainside, let freedom ring!

And if America is to be a great nation, this must become true.

And so let freedom ring from the prodigious hilltops of New Hampshire.

Let freedom ring from the mighty mountains of New York.

Let freedom ring from the heightening Alleghenies of Pennsylvania.

Let freedom ring from the snow-capped Rockies of Colorado.

Let freedom ring from the curvaceous slopes of California.

But not only that:

Let freedom ring from Stone Mountain of Georgia.

Let freedom ring from Lookout Mountain of Tennessee.

Let freedom ring from every hill and molehill of Mississippi."[16]

Martin Luther King's mighty cause, and unswerving resolve to see the plight of African American people changed, cost him his life. But his desperate passion for the cause has seen him etched into 20th Century history as a hero of purpose.

---

16   Taken from A Testament Of Hope: The Essential Writings of Martin Luther King, Jr., ed. James M. Washington

People of a cause, who truly embrace it with all that is within them, often give their life to achieve it.

My prayer is that God will keep the white-hot desire in our hearts for the lost multitudes and to pursue our goal with unstoppable zeal.

Giant killers must be people of a cause much greater than themselves, an all-encompassing global cause.

So many Christians fumble through life without a cause. They live aimlessly. God is calling us to clarify our purpose on the earth and to become filled with white-hot passion to achieve our destiny. Do you know your cause? Are you passionately pursuing your destiny with everything within you? God's desire for our lives is to do,

> *"...exceeding abundantly above all that we ask or think, according to the power that worketh in us"*
> Ephesians 3:20

Purpose, or vision, infuses a person with courage and resolve and causes them to attempt and achieve the impossible.

GIANT KILLERS GO OUT AFTER THE PREY

> *"And David said unto Saul, Thy servant kept his father's sheep, and there came a lion, and a bear, and took a lamb out of the flock: And I went out after him, and smote him, and delivered it out of his mouth: and when he arose against me, I caught him by his beard, and smote him and slew him."*
> 1 Samuel 17:34-35

David demonstrates this great characteristic that giant killers must have. "He went out after" the lion. He did not wait for the beast to come to him.

David went out from the flock to snatch a small lamb from the mouth of "a killing machine". A 400 pound animal with paws set with 0.1 m (4 inch) blades that could tear his flesh to ribbons. It could smash his spine with a single blow. This lion's cheek teeth alone could rip David's body in great chunks.

It was no ordinary lion or cub. It was a maned male of age and strength, almost certainly an old male, cut off and alone, that had fought many battles and was in desperate hunger.[17]

On a recent trip to South Africa I visited a farm where some 30 lions are kept in a large open enclosure. The dominant male is named Mustafa. He is a huge majestic beast whose muscled body is a picture of raw power.

On one occasion a horse somehow got into the enclosure. Within seconds, Mustafa launched upon the terrified animal. With one blow of his huge paw, he broke the horse's back and killed it instantly.

David didn't simply go out after the beast but he seized it by the mane. Can you imagine taking hold of the lion so close to those flashing bared teeth, close enough to smell its breath and see the cold steely look of death in its eyes?

Yet he knew who he was and the greatness of his "Great Shepherd". Seizing this beast of terror, that roared with deafening volume into the loneliness of these desolate hills, David smote him to death.

David did not even contemplate his own safety. He was only concerned about the lamb. The natural mind would say, "Well, it's only one lamb, my father will understand, the lamb is probably dead already." David did not think this way. He rose immediately, unflinchingly, and rushed into action.

One British medical officer in World War I, Captain Noel Godfrey Chavasse, became the most highly decorated warrior in Britain's war history. He didn't even carry a rifle, yet he won the Victoria Cross and bar (second Victoria Cross) and the Military Cross for valour. He just kept going out into the face of artillery and machine gun fire to bring back wounded men. Despite being severely wounded personally on more than one occasion, he would not stop.[18]

Like David after that lamb in the lion's mouth, Chavasse dragged

---

17   It is the females that do the hunting.
18   From The Times newspaper 7th November 2006, "Sporting Braves" by Mark Souster

men out of shell holes, 22.8 m (25 yards) from the enemy trenches. With blood streaming from his own wounds, he brought wounded men back to the lines, in the face of withering machine gun and artillery fire. In one night alone, although wounded, he and other volunteers saved 20 wounded men.

Jesus said, "Go ye into all the world" (Mark 16:15). This is likely what He would say to us now:

"Go into your community and bring back the wounded, go into all the nations with good news of the Kingdom of God. Go out into the no man's land made waste by the Devil and bring back the broken, shattered and defeated."

This is the characteristic of a giant killer that every minister of God must have. He must go out into a savage world with courage and fearless resolve.

The wounded of this world lie in the shell holes of human despair, emotionally and spiritually desperate in the lonely "no-man's land" of the Great War of the Ages. They are caught in the mouth of lions of Hell, carrying them away to the lairs of death or crushed by the paws of hellish bears that smash them with the blows of abuse, despair and hopelessness.

In today's disturbed and troubled world, the Church in most places is a haven of comfort. Certainly the Church is an oasis in a harsh world, but the command of the Lord is, "Go".

"And he said unto them, Go ye into all the world, and preach the gospel to every creature."
Mark 16:15

"Why abodest thou among the sheepfolds, to hear the bleatings of the flocks? For the divisions of Reuben there were great searchings of heart.
Gilead abode beyond Jordan: and why did Dan remain

in ships? Asher continued on the sea shore, and abode in his breaches. Zebulun and Naphtali were a people that jeoparded their lives unto the death in the high places of the field." Judges 5:16-18

In Judges 5, Deborah asks probing questions of Israel's tribes, after a mighty victory over Midian.

Why did the double minded tribe of Reuben have great thoughts of heart and remain in the sheepfolds to hear the bleating of the flocks? Why did Gilead remain on the peaceful side of the river? Why did Dan stay in his ships (just going about daily business)? Why did Asher stay on the comfortable bay sea-shore and stay in the breaches? She then commended Zebulun and Naphtali as tribes that put their lives at risk in the high places of the field.

ZEBULUN AND NAPHTALI

The battles for the high places throughout military history have often been the most ferocious and bloody and victory was seized by the most courageous. God is calling out His Zebuluns and Naphtalis. Too many Christians remain in the security of a safe Christian walk, comfortable and apathetic to a dying world.

Deborah praises the conquering warriors of the battlefield. These were the giant killers that left security to fight in the high places of mortal combat. They did not settle for the comfort and security of a quiet, unchallenged, structured life but chose the mountains of ruthless battle.

The great American Naval hero of the American War of Independence, John Paul Jones, was recorded as saying to Benjamin Franklin, "I want a fast ship because I will always be going into harm's way." His own flag flew on the mast of his ship. It featured a coiled rattlesnake and these words: "Don't step on me."

His exploits were extraordinary as he dismantled, with inferior vessels, the might of the British Navy, the greatest navy on the earth at that time.

I always remember when I received my first invitation to preach the gospel in Pakistan. My first reaction was a nervous knot in my stomach but an excitement at a totally new and unexplored situation overruled any trepidation I may have felt.

I knew no-one from Australia who had done a miracle healing mass crusade in that nation. At the time, I hadn't heard of any international preachers. However, I have since met and known a number who have done brave and wonderful exploits in that great nation.

Our arrival in Pakistan was exhilarating, intimidating and extremely satisfying, like a dive off the high tower into the water far below. Our team went to preach and demonstrate kingdom power amidst the carnage of a world strewn with the devastated, wounded multitudes on a ruthless field of battle, where Satan has set about to smash and shatter and leave people mortally wounded in the no-man's land of total indifference.

Pakistan was a great point of change for me. As multitudes crowded into the YMCA ground in Karachi to hear the gospel and experience God's miracle grace, my heart felt waves of certainty that what we were doing was bringing satisfaction and pleasure to the Lord of the harvest. Oh to please Him who has called us!

In Pakistan, God moved so powerfully. The glory of God whirled and swirled over tens of thousands of people. Cripples walked and extraordinary miracles exploded all about us. Multitudes of lives were impacted profoundly and eternally in just a few life-changing days. The thrill of releasing God's power in these places leaves a sense of satisfaction that cannot be described.

God is calling out people whose desire in these last days is to seize the high places. He is looking for people who will place the call of God before the love of their own lives.

GIANT KILLERS MUST BE PEOPLE OF COURAGE

Australia, although considered a young nation in international endeavours, has built a strong reputation for valour on the field of conflict. It is recognized that in World War I, the Australian Infantry Force, despite making up only 10% of the Allied Force, took an estimated 23% of prisoners and achieved a similar percentage of ground seized.

Australian troops gained a strong reputation for audacious acts of valour. Perhaps it was the era of Australian bushmen and pioneers that brought out this daring edge. At the Hindenburg outpost on 18 September 1918, the Australian 1st and 4th Divisions were given the task of seizing the Hindenburg outpost line. One man, Gerald Sexton, *"went out after the lion."*

"Many men served in the First AIF under an alias. It was only with the announcement of the Victoria Cross that Maurice Vincent Buckley revealed that 'Gerald Sexton' was an alias. Under his true name, Buckley had enlisted on 18 December 1914 and was posted to the 13th Light Horse Regiment. He reached Egypt but returned to Australia with venereal disease and was admitted to Langwarrin Camp on 21 January 1916, was declared a deserter, and was struck off strength on 20 March. He re-enlisted under the alias of 'Gerald Sexton' on 6 May 1916: Gerald was the name of his brother who had died six months earlier, shortly after joining the AIF; Sexton was his mother's maiden name."

"On 18 September, the 13th Battalion set off behind a creeping barrage and cleared several enemy outposts, two of which fell to Buckley's Lewis gun. When a field gun held up one company, he rushed towards it, shot the crew, and raced under machine-gun fire across open ground to put a trench mortar out of action. He then fired into an enemy dugout and captured 30 Germans. By the end of the day, he had rushed at least six machine gun positions, captured a field gun, and taken nearly 100 prisoners. The award of the Victoria Cross for these actions was gazetted under the name Sexton."[19]

God is looking for those who will confront and rush forward against all that Hell can throw against them.

---

19   They Dared Mightily

David's courage and willingness to go out after the prey is our example. As we observe events on the earth that throw nations into chaos, we become more aware that the times spoken of in 2 Timothy 3:1 are upon us:

"This know also, that in the last days perilous times shall come."

"Always attack. Even in defence, attack. The attacking arm possesses the initiative and thus commands the action. To attack makes men brave; to defend makes them timorous. If I learn that an officer of mine has assumed a defensive position on the field, that officer will never hold command under me again."
Alexander the Great

GIANT KILLERS RUN AT THEIR FOE

"And it came to pass, when the Philistine arose, and came and drew nigh to meet David, that David hasted, and ran toward the army to meet the Philistine."
1 Samuel 17:48

These words tell us much about the young shepherd boy. We have already seen his attitude of one who went out after his prey. Again, he didn't wait for the prey to come to him. He hastened and ran toward his enemy. We see his courage and inner certainty of his God-given destiny and purpose. He does not advance timidly or full of doubt. His approach was a purposeful charge at the giant that confronted him.

Some years ago, my mother talked to me of my great uncle Major General George James Rankin who passed away in the late 1950s. She explained to me that he had been a member of the 4th Light Horse Regiment of the first AIF (Australian Infantry Forces) and served in Palestine during the first World War of 1914-1918. As a student of military history, I pricked up my ears. I began to wonder if he had taken part in one of the most audacious charges in military history, the famous charge of the Australian Light Horse on the town of Beersheeba. Here the Turks, under German oversight, held the ancient wells of Abraham, Isaac and Jacob.

This was to be a David and Goliath situation, as 800 Light Horsemen charged headlong into a seemingly impossible mission.

The date was 30 January 1917 in the very place that Abraham had sojourned so long before.

The taking of the objective, Beersheba, and the capture of the wells, originally sunk by Abraham, was supposed to be achieved in the day. Unfortunately, the British commanders had underestimated the strength of the defensive fortifications, weaponry and the dogged defiance of the Turkish force of some 5,000 men. The great British force was totally halted in its advance.

Desperation gripped the field commanders as they gazed at the historical town of Beersheba several miles away. The wells dug in Abraham's day had been contested for generations. This day, 30 January 1917, a British and Allied Force of some 40,000 men were faced with a crisis: the objective of Beersheba was supposedly a simple task achieved in the day.

Water supplies were almost gone and thirst gripped mercilessly their massive force. A force of 4,000 to 5,000 Turks had fortified the ancient place with strong trench, machine gun and artillery batteries and had resisted relentlessly every British advance. Here was the only water for many miles. To seize these wells was critical to save the British force. The victory had to occur before sunset. Yet the Turkish resistance had totally held the British advance.

This was the gateway to the taking of Jerusalem – this prize had to be seized.

The demand late in the day was for "violent assault" by "audacious men" with the most "ardent zeal" and "intense exertion". The demand was for audacity, the action of people with a different spirit.

The task fell to the Australian 4th Light Horse Division and others. These tanned, rugged horsemen with their plumed slouch hats and

reputation as elite warriors assaulted Beersheba with a frontal charge
of 800 men and horses into the direct face of artillery, machine gun
and rifle fire. One man from Rochester, Victoria, Australia who had left
his farm, bringing three magnificent horses with him was instructed
to organise the men into lines and set them into battle position. His
name was Major George Rankin, later Major General George Rankin,
my great uncle.

The 800 plumed horsemen charged across almost one mile of open
ground into the face of artillery and machine gun fire. Like insane,
frenzied fanatics they rode, as the smell of water filled the nostrils of
the thirst crazed walers.[20]

Shells whistled and whirred overhead, bullets fizzled around them
on every side but a prize was there to be seized: destiny, deliverance
and a name that would echo in the halls of valour enveloped them that
day.

Uncle George returned to Australia and pursued a successful career
in politics. At his funeral, eight generals accompanied his coffin on a
gun carriage as he was buried with full military honours.

To me, it seems totally miraculous that the great David and Goliath
situation at Beersheeba almost 100 years ago could possibly have
succeeded but, like David, they charged ferociously into the face of
massive opposition.

So often we skirt about and wait for all the circumstances to be
in our favour before we advance. When we, like David, we know the
cause and the rightness of God's timing, let us charge into the face of
all that rises up against us.

The greatest harvest in human history is ready for fearless warriors to
charge with fearless resolve into the midst. An ancient writer observed:

"Fortune favors the brave."[21]

We need Christian leaders who will inspire and stir the ranks of
Christendom to rise up in the weaponry of the Holy Ghost and assault

20   Wailers were a large, powerful Australian horse bred in New South Wales
known therefore as Walers.

21   Virgil, Aenid, Roman epic poet (70BC-19BC), www.quotationspage.com

the gates of Hell.

It is time for leaders like David to inspire and stimulate sleeping Christian ranks into God's "storm troopers".

DAVID WAS AN INSPIRER OF MEN

History is filled with great generals and leaders who inspired armies to superhuman feats of courage and endurance.

In the great epic movie "Braveheart", William Wallace (Mel Gibson) rode in front of a Scottish army, which was about to leave the Stirling battlefield, intimidated by the size of the British army that was fronted by 300 heavy horse Cavalry. Although it lacks historical integrity, the scene was emotionally stirring.

The sight of these great battle horses and armed knights with massive war lances and the glint of the armour of a far greater, better equipped and numerically superior army had melted the Scottish Army and taken all the fight out of them. The situation demanded a leader who, like David, would swing the mindset of a whole army from mental paralysis to invincible unstoppable might.

As the intimidated and mentally defeated Scottish soldiers began to walk from the field at Stirling, returning to their homes, Wallace rode onto the field, armed with a 2 m (6.56 feet) sword and his face painted blue, his eyes and whole persona set with deadly resolve. The army had dissolved, in its mind all purpose was gone. They were already mentally defeated. The sights of the massive British force and the "heavy horse" Cavalry had drained the fight out of each man.

Wallace then proceeded to assault their mindsets by an impacting speech. With his eyes flashing with righteous indignation and his jaw set in total committed defiance, he shouts:

> **"Sons of Scotland…I am William Wallace and I see a whole army of my countrymen here in defiance of tyranny. You've come to fight as free men and free men you are. What will you do with that freedom? Will you fight?"**

A negative defeated mumble of "no" comes from the army followed by a single represented voice,

> **"Against that, no we will run and we will live.**
> **Aye, fight and you may die, run and you will live at least**
> **a while and dying in your bed, many years from now**
> **would you be willing to trade all the days from this day**
> **for that one chance, just one chance to come back here**
> **and tell our enemies that they may take our lives but**
> **they will never take our freedom."** William Wallace[22]

The mindset of an entire army changed, fear turned to defiance with an attitude that caused a mentally defeated army to rise and crush the English force at Stirling.

We are those who can change mindsets and attitudes by the confident certainty and strength of our words.

Giant killers in the Kingdom of God, like Caleb, Joshua, Moses and David, possess an unshakeable mindset and attitude.

David in one day on the field of Shochoh changed the mindset of an army, a nation and millions of people through the ages. People young and old still stand up on the inside as they relive the story of the defiant courage of a teenage shepherd boy.

Giant killers change the mindsets of whole nations often just through the power of their words. We need to seek every opportunity to impact and influence the mindsets of people around us.

---

22   "Braveheart", Paramount Pictures

GIANT KILLERS SEE THROUGH DIFFERENT EYES

"And David spake to the men that stood by him, saying, What shall be done to the man that killeth this Philistine, and taketh away the reproach from Israel? for who is this uncircumcised Philistine, that he should defy the armies of the living God?" 1 Samuel 17:26

It is amazing that two people can look at the identical series of events and come up with two totally conflicting views. It seems that people see, or certainly interpret, life's events in amazingly different ways. It is said of David as he confronted Goliath that "The army of Israel saw Goliath as too big to fight while David saw him as too big to miss." David saw the reward not the danger. He saw immense opportunity not great peril.

As Israel looked upon the giant and heard his thunderous roaring voice, they trembled and felt "like grasshoppers" before him. David, on the other hand, saw a God-given opportunity to seize his destiny. The Promised Land was missed for 45 years because a nation looked through defeated eyes.

Over the years, I have enjoyed the privilege of knowing the former Australian Test Cricket Captain, Steven Waugh. He is regarded as one of the toughest and strongest-minded players in Australia's history. In the West Indies, Steve batted an innings that inspired his team mates and all of Australia with the raw audacious courage he showed. From a distance of 20.1 m (22 yards), he faced the thunderbolt fast bowlers on a cricket pitch that was under-prepared (in the view of many). This meant that the 0.15 Kg (5½oz) cricket ball reared off the pitch at 150 km per hour (over 90 miles per hour) and put the batsmen at considerable risk. Curtley Ambrose was a giant of a man who thundered the ball down into the pitch so that it reared uncertainly into the ribcage and throat area, which unsettled most batsmen. Steve took the challenge and, despite blow after blow that struck his body, he glared continually at his opponent and mentally took control over his tormentors.

He finished the day physically bruised and battered but had systematically hammered the intimidating attack to the tune of 200 runs, his highest test score.

Extreme fast bowling causes some fear in most batsmen who play the game of cricket. I asked Steve what it was like to be struck by the missile-like bowling of Curtley Ambrose. His words stunned me: "I don't mind it. It helps me to concentrate."

For some fear or self preservation dominates their thinking. In Steven's case it was an aid in concentration.

Israel saw a terrifying giant on the field of battle, a tormentor, an undefeatable opponent. David saw an opportunity and a gift from God that would take him to the next phase of his God-ordained destiny.

How do you view the giants that stand against your destiny?

The giant you face has to be seen in a different light. You must choose how you see him.

Is he there to destroy you or is he a gift from God?

Is he your destroyer or your stepping stone to the next phase of authority and destiny?

Could he have been allowed to come against you in order to bring out in you tenacity in the spirit, courage and resolve to find the giant killer in you?

Could this giant you face be your stepping stone to a place of kingly dominion and supernatural authority like you have never seen before?

The giant may be big, leering, bombarding with incessant messages of self-doubt, fear, confusion and failure. He may be targeting your health, family, business or finance.

This giant is your prey.

We need to see the giants we face in the same way David saw Goliath.

David also asked the probing question:

"What shall be done to the man that killeth this Philistine..." 1 Samuel 17:26

What is the reward?

DEAD GIANTS BRING BIG REWARD

David looked ahead and saw a huge vision of possibility that could come from this momentous opportunity. He didn't see the defeat or his own death. He saw a chance to step into his destiny. David saw this moment in history as his time, when an insignificant shepherd boy could seize life by the throat. He saw reward, economic, political and very personal.

Jesus looked the giant of death and Hell square in the eye for, "the joy that was set before him".[23] For the salvation of multitudes of humanity, He "endured the cross, despising the shame".[24]

For David the reward would prove to be far greater than that offered by King Saul:

> "...*the man who killeth him, (Goliath) the king will enrich him with great riches, and will give him his daughter, and make his father's house free in Israel.*"
> 1 Samuel 17:25

Israel's host only saw what the giant would do to them. David saw what killing the giant would do for him.

How do we view the giants that come against us? Do we ask what they will do to us, our ministry, home or families? Or do we ask what the defeat of them will do for our lives, ministries, homes, families and finances?

David did not view himself as Goliath's prey. He saw himself as God's man born for this moment. He did not see himself like the spies who had gone into view the Promised Land centuries before. They had seen themselves as grasshoppers.

---

23   Hebrews 12:2
24   Hebrews 12:2

"And there we saw the giants, the sons of Anak, which come of the giants: and we were in our own sight as grasshoppers, and so we were in their sight."
Numbers 13:33

The army of Israel saw themselves as grasshoppers before Goliath. Joshua and Caleb could only see the promise of God and the certainty of victory. David saw himself as God's man, "God's storm trooper", and Goliath as his prey and spoil.

How do we see ourselves? The Bible tells us that as a man thinks in his own heart that is who he actually is. We are not who others think we are. We are who we think we are in Christ.

"For as he thinketh in his heart, so is he..." Proverbs 23:7

We must develop a Christ centred mindset because visionaries have shaped history.

"We are not the hunted, but the hunters, God's storm troopers seizing the gates of Hell." Reinhard Bonnke

GIANT KILLERS MUST POSSESS AN UNSHAKEABLE MINDSET

One of David's early characteristics seems to be an unshakeable mindset in the face of fierce opposition. I heard a preacher once say:

"There are plenty of people with a vision but few with the resolve to bring it to pass. The great feats of history were always performed by people of resolve."

Alexander the Great by the age of 20 had developed an unshakeable mindset, that he would conquer Persia.

Recently, I spent time in the humble war rooms in London where Sir Winston Churchill and his wife had stayed during the London Blitz of World War II. Here, I could picture Sir Winston Churchill planning the invasion of France while the bombs reigned down and pulverised the city above. The rooms were not totally bombproof. A direct hit could have come through but Churchill's mind was set like a bulldog that eyed a tasty bone.

I could feel the unshakeable resolve of Sir Winston and the British people when certain defeat seemed to stare them in the face. Although the city of London was in ruins and wave after wave of Luftwaffe bombers darkened the skies, Churchill's defiant unshakeable words caused a whole nation to take on an attitude that marked them as the "bulldog" nation. Churchill's words echoed by radio across the nation:

"We will never, never, surrender."

Victory over the giants we face will occur firstly in the "spirit of our minds".

David saw through different eyes and established a clear mindset.

David's vision extended far beyond the reward offered by the king, or even the fame that would come to him: for the destruction of Goliath.

He saw a picture, even larger than the destruction of the massive Philistine force that stood arrayed against them. He saw the impact of this battle sending giant ripples across the Earth that declared the might of the God of Israel. His vision as a youth was a global vision. Perhaps he even recognized that his exploit on the field that day would echo across the Earth for millenniums to come.

> *"This day will the LORD deliver thee into mine hand; and I will smite thee, and take thine head from thee; and I will give the carcases of the host of the Philistines this day unto the fowls of the air, and to the wild beasts of the earth; that all the earth may know that there is a God in Israel."* 1 Samuel 17:46

Alexander the Great made the following statement to his General Ptolomy who would later become Pharoah of Egypt:

"When deliberating, think in campaigns and not in battles; in wars and not campaigns; in ultimate conquest and not wars."[25]

Sportsmen use the term self belief. We are those that have the "in-Jesus" belief. We must see ourselves as He sees us and then act accordingly.

We must know what He says about you and me. We can choose how we think!

WHAT SHOULD BE DONE WITH THE GIANT'S HEAD?

"And David took the head of the Philistine, and brought it to Jerusalem; but he put his armour in his tent."
1 Samuel 17:54

Have you ever wondered what became of Goliath's head? The armour was placed in David's tent as a trophy, a reminder of his great moment of triumph and a statement of life's great turning points when he took his opportunity and stepped out with courage in God's great arena of faith.

But what of the giant's large head, with the smooth stone from the brook still embedded in the skull?

I always picture David dropping it at the feet of King Saul or placing it on a pike as a trophy before Israel's army but neither of these situations occurred. David carried the head into Jerusalem. At this point of time, the city was Jebus, controlled by the Jebusites ("polluters" of the Holy Place). I picture David walking up the main street, carrying the massive severed head, a grizzly reminder to the whole city that a giant killer was in town. Like Arnold Schwarzenegger, this was likely to be David's statement to his future stronghold: "I'll be back". I wonder whether he carried the head to the door of government and laid it down as a statement: "I have killed this giant and I am coming back to make this my castle, my city, my mountain and the city of my great God who always leads me in triumph".

David's procession into Jerusalem may not have had the pomp of a Roman triumphant procession. After all, he was only a teenage shepherd boy who didn't even own a suit of armour. He didn't have a plumed, inscribed helmet or splendid robes but, as he carried the bloodied head of the terrifying warrior, his march into Jerusalem, flanked by warriors inspired by his raw valour, must have sent chilling shockwaves through the Jebusites and all the enemies of Israel.

David's bold march before the Jebusites as he held the statement of his great victory was a picture of a much greater triumph centuries later. After his mighty resurrection from the dead, Jesus led the defeated tormentor of the ages before the entire arrayed spirit world, angels and demons alike. Satan's head had been crushed by the Master's heel, his dominion smashed, captivity loosed and the very name of Jesus sent chills of terror through the ranks. Here was an open stripping of authority and total dominion.

David had walked into Jerusalem with a declaration, "I shall return". The time came when he did come to his city. Despite the cry of the Jebusite inhabitants, "You can't come in here", he took the city.

In the same way, Jesus paraded Satan before those who claimed the world system. He also declared His intention to return and seize His entire inheritance starting at the same city, Jersusalem.

The world system cried out to Jesus, "You can't have this world." Nevertheless, he is preparing now to seize what is His.

David paraded his statement of divine triumph before the Jebusites.

There are times, after God has given us a great victory over a giant foe, that we should parade that severed head of control before principalities and powers to declare our God-given authority and strength as sons and daughters of the Living God.

Perhaps you have had a massive victory in your life over disease or abuse. Perhaps you have been delivered out of alcohol or drug addiction or have conquered a financial giant or overcome a giant who has held you bound for years. You must parade that captured head openly through the streets and airways of our Jebusite-held towns and cities. Record your testimony, produce CDs or DVDs and distribute them. Take every opportunity to flaunt and brag of your great and mighty God. Maybe it is time to write your testimony of victory in book form and see it distributed to the nations. The Bible tells us the awesome power of our testimony causes an overcoming of the Devil.[26]

I wonder if the severed head of Goliath had been carried to Ekron, Shaaraim and even to Gath in the pursuit of the Philistines before it was triumphantly carried through the streets of Jerusalem.

It is wonderful when we can parade our giants' heads through the places where they once controlled us.

I have a friend in New York who was a gang leader and serious drug dealer but now has a powerful church on the street that he once walked for Satan. The last time I preached for him was during a time when they had a chain of prayer, fasting and worship, 24 hours per day, that ran for 40 days.

Most of the leaders and deacons in that church had stalked those streets as Satan's agents and found Jesus in prison.

Now a constant procession of triumph for Jesus filled those streets.

The Bible tells us that Jesus always, "leads us in triumph".[27]

We are being paraded as trophies of triumph before terrified demons and amazed angels.

The real understanding of the triumphant procession was shown to us in ancient Rome. They were seen as her generals returned from great conquests. The generals rode in splendour in magnificently prepared chariots pulled by superb horses with extravagant pomp and music. They entered Rome, with the armoured legions, to the deafening cry of the multitudes. The legions, in their polished magnificent armour, plumed helmets and imposing shields, marched with thousands of

26   Revelation 12:11
27   2 Corinthians 2:14

prisoners in chains. Opposing generals were displayed to the masses, followed by exotic animals and dancers from conquered regions that brought added colour and excitement to this lavish and brutal statement of the Empire's might.

The mighty Roman Empire has faded now into the dust and ruins of the ages. Her might and power is still seen in the ruins left behind after the Gauls sacked and pillaged the proud city. Around the world, her ruined amphitheatres and temples talk of splendid pomp and great conquests won but the triumphant processions are over. The processions of Hitler, Napoleon and the generals of history fade to dust but the great, onward, ever-moving procession of Christ's triumph grows ever larger, more vocal, louder and louder in deafening praise and we are part of it.

Like David of old carrying Goliath's head God is sending us into cities and nations crying out:

"Christ's giant killers are here. His Kingdom power is in her. Step aside, we are carrying giants' heads and we have only just begun to seize our destiny."

GIANT KILLERS KNOW THE ANOINTING

"Then Samuel took the horn of oil, and anointed him in the midst of his brethren: and the Spirit of the LORD came upon David from that day forward." 1 Samuel 16:13

"Then answered one of the servants, and said, Behold, I have seen a son of Jesse the Bethlehemite, that is cunning in playing, and a mighty valiant man, and a man of war, and prudent in matters, and a comely person, and the LORD is with him." 1 Samuel 16:18

Here was David's greatest strength. The Lord was with him. God's mighty anointing rested upon his life.

For years I have preached across the continents that the single greatest privilege we have is to be able to declare like Isaiah:

> *"The spirit of the Lord God is upon me; because the Lord hath anointed me..."* Isaiah 61:1

More than upon us we are baptised into and clothed with the absolute power and presence of God Himself.

I love Reinhard Bonnke's teachings on the baptism in the Holy Spirit. He talks of John the Baptist at the Jordan and his introduction of Jesus to His followers (Matthew 3:11):

> **"I baptise you in water for the remission of sins but He (Jesus) will immerse you in liquid fire."**
> Reinhard Bonnke

Jesus truly is the Baptiser in the mighty life-transforming power of God Himself. John G. Lake, the great apostle to Africa, made wonderful statements describing the awesome impact of God's mighty power through us and in us:

> **"Sin, sickness, death under His feet, Hell itself taken captive and obedient to His Word, every enemy of mankind throttled, bound, chained by the Son of God. Mankind joined to Him by the Holy Ghost in living triumph. Why if I receive of the Spirit of Jesus Christ, of the Christ who is, I receive the Spirit of victory and power and might and dominion, of grace, of love, of all the blessed estate of which Jesus is now the conscious master. All these things He gives the Christian through imparting to him the Holy Ghost."**
> **What a privilege: "quickened together with Christ"[28], and that we are "one spirit"[29] with the Eternal King. This is power that the giants of life cannot conquer.**

---

28   Ephesians 2:5
29   I Corinthians 6:17

David, like the great men and women of history who performed great exploits for God and have known and recognized who they are in God and what they carry, David knew that what he carried in his life was the indomitable, awesome, unstoppable power of God. No Goliath that the Devil could raise could stand against God's anointed man.

In Ephesians, we read the Apostle's constant prayer for the saints at Ephesus and also for us that we might truly know the mighty unstoppable power of God that rests on us:

> *"The eyes of your understanding being enlightened, that we might know what is the hope of his calling, and what the riches of the glory of his inheritance in the saints, And what is the exceeding greatness of his power to us ward who believe, according to the working of his mighty power, Which he wrought in Christ, when he raised him from the dead, and set him at his own right hand in the heavenly places,"* Ephesians 1:18-20

In Ephesians chapter 1, Paul prays that we might see the unlimited magnitude of His power that is directed towards every believer but, in chapter 3, he declares that we might be:

> *"...filled with all the fulness of God."*[30]

Then he goes on to declare that as a result of this mighty infilling we are able to:

> *"do exceeding abundantly above all that we ask or think,"*[31]

> *"[That you may really come] to know [practically, through experience for yourselves] the love of Christ,*

---

30   Ephesian 3:10b
31   Ephesians 3:20

which far surpasses mere knowledge [without experience]; that you may be filled [through all your being] unto all the fullness of God [may have the richest measure of the divine Presence, and become a body wholly filled and flooded with God Himself]!

Now to Him Who, by (in consequence of) the [action of His] power that is at work within us, is able to [carry out His purpose and] do superabundantly, far over and above all that we [dare] ask or think [infinitely beyond our highest prayers, desires, thoughts, hopes, or dreams]"
Ephesians 3:19-20 (Amplified Bible)

Paul had a revelation of a God who was able to do exceedingly, abundantly, beyond anything he could ask or think because of the power at work within him.

Paul declares to us his ongoing passion that we are aware of exactly who we are in Christ and the unlimited, incalculable, dimension of God's mighty power that is directed towards and flowing out of His believing people.

Paul is writing here to the Ephesians who had seen the arm of the Lord laid bare in a show of God's power that was so mighty that it was destroying the pagan worship of the goddess Diana. Ephesus was the centre of the worship of Artemis, or Diana, and certainly a major centre for the making of idols to the goddess. Paul was destroying the trade in idolatry by the mighty anointing that rested upon him. They had seen an astonishing move of God in Ephesus that began with 12 new converts recently baptized in the baptism of John. So great was the revival power, which began from the school room of Tyrannus with these men, that the whole west coast province of Asia Minor, both Jew and Greek, heard the gospel.

It is estimated that, in Ephesus alone, the church may have reached 40,000 people in those two years. Paul was carrying an anointing of God so strong, that handkerchiefs and aprons carried from his body, when laid upon the sick, possessed and diseased, were a catalyst for extraordinary miracles.

David was anointed with a giant killing anointing, as are we. The anointing that is upon our lives is mighty in God to the demolition of strongholds. We are filled with the greatest power the world has ever known.

Paul writes to the Ephesians, that, despite being part of a huge revival and having seen extraordinary miracles at his hand, it was time for them to see for themselves who they were in Christ, what they could do and be for him and to know what was the "exceeding greatness"[32], or the unlimited magnitude, of power that was towards them and is towards us today.

He declares that this power, which is without limit towards us, is the same mighty power that raised Jesus from the dead. This is the mighty power that caused the great giant of death to bow the knee and surrender its prey.

In Acts Chapter 1, we read of Christ's 40 days of amazing appearances following his resurrection. We read of "many infallible proofs"[33], as He showed Himself to his astounded followers.

It has been very satisfying over the past 35 years to see consistently wonderful displays of God's power across the nations.

One that stands out occurred at the conclusion of our vacation some years ago.

It was a balmy summer night in a coastal country town in New South Wales, Australia and our family had driven some eight hours from a holiday in Queensland. I had agreed to preach for a close friend of mine that night.

As I was extremely weary after driving for those eight hours, I didn't really feel like preaching. The meeting in a town hall had attracted a good crowd and I endeavoured to preach as well as possible, despite my weariness.

I recall that it was a tough night to preach. The atmosphere in the hall seemed flat and somewhat void of the power of God.

Suddenly, a lady rushed from the back of the building, screaming. She clutched a young child to her chest. She rushed to me and pushed the child into my arms.

---

32   Ephesians 1:19
33   Acts 1:3

Somewhat bewildered, I stopped, looked about and realized that here I was, in front of a now most interested crowd, with a dead child in my arms. The child had died about 15 minutes previously. Attempts to revive it had failed. I held a beautiful child with as giant of death leered and brooded. This was a very lonely and unnerving moment.

I asked the congregation to stand and shout words and prayers of triumph. We stood and shouted, as we commanded and declared life. How we underestimated the awesome power of our words.

We read that faith like a tiny mustard seed, expressed in triumphant words, will move a mountain.

Suddenly, the giant's hold on its prey snapped. I felt the awesome power of God and then heard breath fill the baby's lungs. The little dead eyes opened and sparked with the life of God. The giant of death gave way to God's mighty anointing.

The Apostle Paul really knew and understood the awesome thing that he carried. To the Corinthians, he declared:

> *"And I was with you in weakness, and in fear, and in much trembling, And my speech and my preaching was not with the enticing words of man's wisdom, but in demonstration of the Spirit and of power."*
> 1Corinthians 2:3-4

Paul recognised that he carried the power of God to truly demonstrate the word. This gospel is to be a demonstrated gospel.

David understood what he carried. Perhaps as he strode out onto the field to confront his massive Philistine opponent, he may have recalled an incident that had occurred many years previously. The Ark of the Covenant, the symbol of God's power and the piece of sacred furniture upon which God's glory was manifested, had been seized by the Philistines. Jewish history intimates that Goliath, as a young man, had led the victorious army that carried the Ark away to the cities of Philistia.

The Ark of God had been lost to the same enemy that now confronted him. Israel was suffering from the Philistines' reproach.

The Philistines had marched the Ark through their cities. They had derided and mocked the God of Israel in a way similar to the arrogant, defiant shouts of Goliath as he marched up and down before Israel's army for 40 days.

Perhaps, as David looked intently at Goliath, the giant statue of the Philistine god Dagon came to his mind. Perhaps he saw the Ark of God, small in size, yet the meeting place of God's unlimited power placed in seeming defeat before Dagon in his temple. He was now God's anointed as he stood before the giant embodiment of all of Philistia's demonic arrogance.

Perhaps in his mind, he saw that massive god crash, face down in obedience, to the glory of God that manifested between the Cherubim's wings. He may have seen that giant head of Dagon, violently break off and roll across the floor and the hands likewise break off at the wrists. Perhaps it was the picture of Dagon's demise and the severing of his head that prompted him to sever Goliath's head. It is a common belief that Dagon's image was inscribed on the front of Goliath's armour.

Now another giant, another defiant impostor like Dagon, would crash at the presence of God's anointed man. This day on the field of battle, the giant Goliath would have his head of control severed and his sword of intimidation seized by God's anointed man. His intimidating voice would be silenced forever.

Goliaths of disease, debt, defeat and death still fall prostrate before the manifested power of God.

Some time ago, we conducted crusade meetings in Port Moresby, Papua New Guinea. On the Sunday morning before the mass meetings I preached at my close friend's church.

The worship was electric and a great sense of anticipation filled the air. The power of the Lord was explosively ready to smash Dagons. I preached a faith message and we began to minister healing to the people. I urged them, in the presence of God's power, to act on their faith.

One man was carried into the meeting on a stretcher. He was paralysed and bedridden for six months. Cancer began in his feet, spread through his body now totally paralysed him. He appeared to be close to death. As we challenged the people to act on their faith, I observed people stand around him as his hands and legs began to move. As he was helped to his feet, we saw huge growths under them as he hobbled forward. We watched in awe as the feet lowered till they went flat to the floor. Then he began to take confident steps. The congregation rose as one to shout as the Goliath of cancer gave way to the mighty, tangible anointing of God that filled the air.

It was astonishing to watch those ballooned, cancer-filled feet return to normal before our very eyes. It seemed to me that this miracle was just like the story in Luke 5, when the paralysed man was lowered through the roof. The same Jesus of the Gospels manifested His power in our midst. The following night we were amazed that he came by taxi to the National Stadium. As he walked across the platform freely, his face shone with joy, as the crowd cheered and clapped.

A deadly giant had been smashed by the power of our Living God.

The greatest joy for me personally as a minister of our great God is to watch people encounter His tangible reality in salvation, healing and deliverance.

Recently, I ministered a series of healing and miracle meetings in New Zealand.

The power of God flowed mightily on this night. I began to walk out into the crowd to lay hands on different individuals as I went up the aisle.

I felt strongly drawn to lay my hands on the head of a middle-aged gentleman. As I did I felt urged by the Lord to ask if someone nearby had an allergy to gluten (wheat) products. The same man said, "That's me", and immediately the power of God came upon him, which caused him to tremble violently. I didn't realise at the time that a drop-saw had once fallen upon him and cut through his arm. Tendons and muscles had been severed and movement in his hand was very greatly reduced.

As the tangible power of God flooded through him, his hand was totally restored. The power of God is tangible. It is as real as electricity and the air we breath. It can be felt, seen and even heard, such as on the day of Pentecost.

The anointing of God takes hold of ordinary people and enables them to do the impossible.

In I Samuel 10, we read that the Spirit of the Lord would come on Saul and he would be changed into another man.

When the anointing of God came on Samson, he became an invincible one-man army.

The anointing of God is indeed tangible. It flows through people, through their clothes and even in one case through a man's bones. A dead man thrown into Elisha's tomb touched the prophet's dead bones and was quickened to life by the power of God that was still resident in his corpse.

Just as people who touched Jesus' clothes were miraculously healed, so Paul's handkerchiefs and aprons laid on the sick resulted in miracles. Not only were the handkerchiefs and aprons a point of faith contact but they were permeated with the glory of God that flowed from the apostle's body.

GIANT KILLERS - PEOPLE OF PRAYER

David certainly understood the power of prayer. In the Psalms we discover his passion to seize hold of God.

> *"O God, thou art my God; early will I seek thee: my soul thirsteth for thee, my flesh longeth for thee in a dry and thirsty land, where no water is: To see thy power and thy glory, so as I have seen thee in the sanctuary."*
> Psalms 63:1-2

> *My soul, said David, "followeth hard after thee (God)".*[34]

Here is the passion of a giant killer. His soul, in fact his whole being, was desperate for God.

When the giant came against my family, the only place I knew to go was into intense prayer.

---

[34]   Psalms 63:8

I read in Scripture how King Hezekiah, in critical circumstances, set his face to the wall and cried out to God. Each day, I set my face to the kitchen wall, hours per day, cried out to God and fasted. Darkness and despair seemed to swallow me up but, as I fervently sought God with persistence and purposeful prayer, the battle swung and I sensed the steel of God's power rise in absolute defiance of all that the enemy brought against me. I began to understand our wrestling match described by Paul in his letter to the Ephesians.

> *"For we wrestle not against flesh and blood, but against principalities, against powers, against the rulers of the darkness of this world, against spiritual wickedness in high places."* Ephesians 6:12

The word "wrestle" is the Greek word pal.[35] It refers to the ancient combat contest, which was ruthless and brutal. Wrestlers could break a man's spine or gouge out his opponent's eyes. The total aim of the contest was to bring the opponent either to a place of surrender or to the place where he could be pinned down by the neck and totally subdued.

My prayer at this time seemed to gush with forceful strength out of areas of my life that I didn't even understand. It seemed that, in the agonizing struggle, God mined deep wells and reached down into the depths of my being to search out a ferocious warrior who could not be stopped or halted. It seems that, in the hardest fiery trials that we face under assault by giants, our attitude of strong confession and fervent, aggressive, unstoppable prayer creates a furnace where we are honed and shaped into sharp threshing instruments.

Prayer in critical times, when giants face us, seems to come from the depths of our being, as Paul describes with, "groanings which cannot be uttered".[36] This indeed was my experience as I seized hold of God in total dependence.

We read of Epaphras, a mighty man who was "always labouring fervently…in prayers"[37] for the saints at Colossae.

35   Strong's G3823
36   Romans 8:26
37   Colossians 4:12

The term "always labouring fervently" is very powerful in the original Greek language. "Always" means at all times or continually while "labouring fervently" is very significant. The Greek word here is "agnizomai"[38] which generally refers to intense training, often brutal in the training of warriors and athletes for the ancient games. The word encapsulates the meaning of great striving and struggle in intense contention with an adversary. It also describes the painstaking effort required for elite standing as a warrior athlete. It has the understanding of agonising, totally-focussed commitment.

It is this intense fervent prayer that triggered the great revivals of history and indeed brings the great breakthroughs today.

This great crisis in my life caused me to understand the impact of Jacob's great night of intense prayer at Jabbok.

When Jacob came to the crossroad of his life[39] he found himself at a place called Jabbok, (which means pouring forth in Hebrew)[40]. He could move neither forward nor back. His usurping past had caught up with him. He now faced giants that had risen from his selfish and manipulative past.

He was pursued by Laban his father-in-law because his wives had stolen the family gods and moved towards the land of his brother Esau, who he had defrauded of his birthright.

He was confronted by the giants of fear, doubt, guilt and confusion and wondered for his own life.

He came to a massive wrestling match with the angel of the Lord, perhaps a Christophany. Why would a man of God wrestle with God? The answer to this is best summed up in the angel's question:

"What is thy name?" Genesis 32:27

The Hebrew word for name is Shem[41] and it speaks of "conspicuous position, character, renown or report". God had put his finger on a giant in Jacob's own life, the evil of his own character.

---

38   Strong's G75
39   Genesis 32:
40   Strong's H2999
41   Strong's H8034

The truth is, that on this night of torrid physical wrestling, Jacob's character came into battle with the God he served. The giants of his own character had come face to face with God's great call and purpose. Sometimes the giants we face are part of our own nature and personality.

It was a torrid, bruising, exhausting struggle that left him crippled. But the giant that had to be destroyed was that of his own supplanting, twisting character and nature.

Jacob firstly recognised the giants in front (Esau) and behind (Laban) then passionately seized hold of his God. As he wrestled through the night he was totally transformed in his own character.

His name was changed from "supplanter" to "Prince of God". His nature was changed from a twister to one with power with God and with men. Jacob himself called Jabbok by a new name Peniel, which means "the face of God"[42].

Confrontation with giants can be the catalyst for a whole new place with God. Our response to seemingly insurmountable opposition will see us rise with him to greater and greater places of strength and intimacy or see us flounder and wallow in defeat and self pity.

"You can't be pitiful and powerful at the same time."
Joyce Meyer

There are seasons in our journey with God where the only place we can go is wholeheartedly after Him. The most significant time in Jacob's life occurred at Jabbok. Even the name of the place gives us an understanding of Jacob's encounter. The name Jabbok means "pouring forth". With his enraged father-in-law pursuing him and his betrayed brother in front he wrestled through the night with God.

It is in these desperate wrestlings that our nature, ambitions and fears of giant opposition are confronted by God's mighty power and we are transformed.

As Jacob wrestled, it began with his own strength but, when his leg was crippled, it was his opponent who began to bear his weight. With

---

42   Strong's H6439

the sinew of his thigh torn, the one he wrestled with began to bear his weight. With the thigh crippled and almost certainly in intense pain, he could only cling on to his opponent. His intense, selfish, controlling nature became dependent on God.

I have always enjoyed this Scripture:

> *"And from the days of John the Baptist until now the kingdom of heaven suffereth violence, and the violent take it by force."* Matthew 11:12

I particularly like the way it is worded in the Amplified Bible:

> *"And from the days of John the Baptist until the present time, the kingdom of heaven has endured violent assault, and violent men seize it by force, [as one precious prize—a share in the heavenly kingdom is sought with the most ardent zeal and intense exertion]."* Matthew 11:12 (Amplified Bible)

This Scripture always seemed to be contradictory to some other Scriptures that I enjoyed.

> *"Fear not, little flock; for it is your Father's good pleasure to give you the kingdom."* Luke 12:32

We are told that we have free and bold access into the Throne Room. Why then do we read of the Kingdom being seized with violent force, "ardent zeal" and "intense exertion"?

I put this before the Lord and this was the conclusion that filled my mind and spirit:

Certainly, we have free access to God's throne at any time. However, Satan constantly endeavours to raise circumstances and giant opposition to hinder us and keep us from intimate strength of relationship with God. Giants seem to rise as dark sentinels to hinder, restrict and dilute the intimacy of our relationship with God and our Kingdom impact.

Entrance into God's presence is freely obtained but passionate, intensely-focussed Christians violently smash through every giant obstacle from Hell, firmly convinced that nothing can separate them from God's presence.

No giant, no matter how large or intimidating, will ever keep a Christian warrior from an intimate throne-dwelling relationship with God or from the full expression of his holy calling.

The giant that stepped into our world drove me into a place of agonizing, passionate and desperate prayer that was stronger than I had ever known.

I have always loved prayer more than anything in life. Looking back over 35 years serving the Lord, the highlights of that time have been the weeks alone with God in outback Australia fervently seeking the face of God. David declares in Psalm 121:1,

> *"I will lift up mine eyes unto the hills, from whence cometh my help."* Psalms 121:1

It wasn't the hills that provided strength to David but the intimacy of relationship with God that he forged in the hills around Bethlehem. We will pursue more of this as we look at the preparation of a giant killer.

We began this chapter looking at Psalm 63, which is a potent insight into David's prayer life. It was likely written in the wilderness of Judah, which is a brutal, unforgiving, uncultivated tract of land on the eastern side of the territory of Judah.

How often in brutal, lonely and unforgiving environments have men and women seized hold of God in prayer? Often it has been out of their own helpless desperation, when life looks hopeless, that they have found the mighty rivers of supernatural power.

This was the same tract of land from which John the Baptist emerged with blazing eyes and words that pierced the hearts of a nation. It was from this same wilderness tract that Jesus emerged in the fullness of the Spirit ready to impact eternity.

Perhaps now you find yourself in a place of great challenge, fear, persecution, loneliness, rejection or overwhelming self doubt. Perhaps, in God's economy, He has allowed you to come to this point knowing that within you is a courageous, tenacious warrior stirred to total transformation of character and power with God and man.

As we will read later, out of desolate wilderness places alone with God, men and women have emerged in nation-shaking Holy Ghost power.

This psalm was written in the wilderness by King David at a time of great personal grief and opposition, almost certainly at the time of the betrayal inflicted upon him by his own son Absalom. The giants of family crisis are often the most ferocious. Here David faced the giant of betrayal by his own son.

Here we feel the groan and cries emerging from the depths of his being.

> *"O God, (Hebrew 'elohiym meaning supreme God[43]) thou art my God; early will I seek thee: my soul thirsteth for thee, my flesh longeth for thee in a dry and thirsty land, where no water is; To see thy power and thy glory, so as I have seen thee in the sanctuary."* Psalm 63:1-2

Here is the impassioned cry of a man in turmoil of heart and soul laying hold of the immovable, supreme, fortress God. The term early will I seek thee (Hebrew word shachar[44]) embraces the following concepts: to be up early and diligently at the task. Strong's Concordance puts it this way: "to be up early at any task (with the implication of earnestness…to search for with painstaking". It seems even more to be an agonising desperation.

David does not cry out, "God meet my need!" Instead, his impassioned declaration is, "my soul thirsteth for thee." It's you, Lord, that I have to have. He declares that his entire being is longing (Hebrew word kamahh[45] to pine after, to faint with longing for). "It's you I have to have Lord!" is the plea of David.

43   Strong's H430
44   Strong's H7836
45   Strong's H3642

In his chaotic situation, David diligently declares to God his spiritually slaked soul and thirsty being desperately desires to feel and see His mighty power and to be embraced by His supreme and almighty strength. Intimacy with God was his greatest desire as he faced the soul-crushing fury of this situation.

Matthew Henry says of these verses that David, "stirs up himself to take hold on God". When all Hell breaks out this has to be the objective of every giant killer.

When great giants come, where must the giant killer go? In 2 Chronicles chapter 20 we see godly King Jehoshaphat confront an army of Ammonites, Moabites and those of Mount Seir (Edom) that come to annihilate the nation. Jehoshaphat became very afraid but then set himself to seek the Lord. I love that. From fear he set himself. He set himself with a proclaimed fast to seek the Lord.

Jehoshaphat's reaction and action is powerfully summarised in verse 3. I like the way it reads in the Amplified Bible:

"Then Jehoshaphat feared, and set himself [determinedly, as his vital need] to seek the Lord; he proclaimed a fast in all Judah." 2 Chronicles 20:3 (Amplified Bible)

Jehoshaphat firstly showed himself to be normal. He was gripped with intense fear. His reaction of fear was channelled into intense personal prayer and then a call for the nation to move into fasting.

"...proclaimed a fast throughout all Judah."
2 Chronicles 20:3b

Jehoshaphat's keys to triumph over an overwhelming army were:
1. He refused to allow fear to dominate so he set himself to seek the face of God.
2. He recognised his total dependence on God and expressed his own lack of power against such a host.
3. He proclaimed a fast both, for himself and the whole nation.

4. He powerfully declared and confessed to God the mighty strength of the promises.

These were the keys that I began to adopt. I had to settle my fears taking them captive[46]. I had to consciously take my emotions captive and then set my face to touch God, to purposefully and single-mindedly throw myself in total dependence on Him.

CONFRONTATIONS WITH GIANTS DEMAND STRONG DECISIONS OF THE WILL

Like Jehoshaphat, I entered an extended time of fasting. This practice of denial of food for a season plays a very significant part throughout the Scripture.

Fasting can never be a works program but is God's great way of enabling us to express our total dependence on Him. It is a faith means of saying to God, "I have nothing natural with which to fight this giant. I set myself in total dependence upon You and Your Word".

In my experience, fasting causes me to really focus all my attention on God's greatness. I pray during these times that, instead of my natural food being absorbed into my life, that the spiritual food of His word would be absorbed supernaturally. Experientially, I find after 10 days or so, God's word opens to me, with a fresh sense of revelation and power and I am personally brought into a strong place of focus with God. I don't try to buy God's favour but to align myself with His purposes and prepare spiritually and mentally to stand powerfully for Him.

As this crisis hit my home and family, I had to do all in my power to keep my gaze totally on the God,

> *"who raises the dead and calls those things that be not as though they were."* Romans 4:17

---

46   2 Corinthians 10:5

I had to keep my eyes, ears and emotions set on "the Greater One".

I spent days fasting and declaring the greatness of God, pushing through the soul-deadening assaults that came in waves, day after day, as I fought through the collateral damage all around our family.

In Scripture, fasting plays a very significant role in many varying scenarios.

- In Matthew 6:16-20, it is revealed as one of three things that God openly rewards: prayer, giving of alms and fasting.
- Moses fasted for two periods of 40 days and nights when he ascended into the fiery glory of God.
- Elijah fasted 40 days on Mount Horeb.
- Jesus, immediately after His baptism in the Jordan River, was driven by the Spirit into the wilderness to be tested by the Devil. Going in the fullness of the Spirit He fasted 40 days and returned in the "power of the spirit"[47].
- It is interesting that the three who fasted 40 days all appeared on the Mount of Transfiguration: Jesus, Moses and Elijah. Fasting and mountaintop experiences with Christ seem to consistently go together.
- Daniel fasted for 21 days waiting on God to bring him clear revelation.
- Nehemiah fasted when he heard of the "affliction and reproach" that came on those who had escaped captivity and who lived in the rubble of Jerusalem.[48]
- Ezra fasted to show God Israel's dependence on Him, as sacred gold and silver temple vessels were brought back through a land of bandits and enemies.[49]
- David fasted often.
- Paul declared that he was in fastings often (2 Corinthians 11:27).
- Fasting and prayer preceded the sending out of the apostles on missionary journeys.
- Jesus declared that some demons are only dislodged by prayer and fasting.

---

47   Luke 4:14
48   Nehemiah 1:2, 3
49   Ezra 8:21,22

This practice was vital throughout the Old Testament and is significant to the New Testament also.

FASTING
A GATEWAY TO THE SUPERNATURAL

At this point, I will change direction briefly and share some of the awesome things that I have discovered during many long periods of fasting and prayer.

I was a young Christian when I first began the adventure of fasting. I don't use the word adventure lightly. I believe absolutely that fasting helps us to enter places of supernatural intimacy and authority.

After I had been a Christian for only a few months, I began to read books that revealed the prayer and fasting lives of many of the great apostles of power in ages past. I began to read the fasting and prayer life of Jesus. I read that, after Jesus had been baptized by John, He was driven by the Holy Spirit into the wilderness and for 40 days fasted, prayed and was tested by the Devil.

I began to fast two days per week as an expression of dependence on God for intimacy with Him. These days of fasting developed into weeks where I would ask God to exchange my natural food for the food of His word. I asked that, instead of absorbing food into my body, He would absorb the food of His word into my spirit.

I found fasting a means of truly expressing my hunger for Him. It was a sacred and precious thing, not a legalistic means of twisting God's arm. That will take a person right out of the realm of faith.

I know that God began to give me wonderful revelation on this subject. Let's look at some of the things He showed me:

1. He challenged me powerfully from Scripture: "Was it actually for Me?" Is fasting based around intimacy with Him?
2. He warned me sternly, "Do not try to buy My power." I became aware that Simon the sorcerer had tried to buy God's power with money and was warned that his soul was in great danger.[50] These words came into my spirit, "What is the difference between buying

---

50   Acts 8

My power with money or with food?" I took the point.

3. He took me in Acts to one of the most significant events in human history: the outpouring of the Holy Spirit on the Gentiles. He showed me Peter sitting on the rooftop about to enjoy his meal that was being prepared in the house. Suddenly he saw in a vision a huge cloth filled with Gentile food lowered down before him. The Lord then commanded him to eat, which stunned Peter. It is interesting that for days Cornelius had fasted from his Gentile food seeking answers from God. Incredibly, the thing he had denied himself in the natural was revealed in a vision that would shape the earth.[51] The Lord said to me that, as we sow our natural food, He can take it and change it into His supernatural food. I have always seen fasting in that light.

4. Following these thoughts, I made a decision to sow heavily in the spirit and began to contemplate fasting as a tithe. There are 365 days in a year, so a tithe is 36.5 days. I thought let's round it off to 40 days and commit the first 40 days of the year to God as a time of intimacy, preparation and seed. That was my practice for a number of years. Perhaps it is time to do it again.

There is an intensity of prayer that rises up within us when trials and trauma come. The challenge is to maintain that awesome intensity of prayer to seek and passionately embrace our God when no great trials face us.

We read in Scripture, and in history, of warriors of prayer. Paul writes to the saints at Colossae about a humble prayer warrior Epaphras. Of this man, Paul says, he is:

> "...always labouring fervently for you in prayers, that ye may stand perfect and complete in all the will of God." Colossians 4:12

This is the prayer life of a giant killer.

---

51   Acts 10:1-16

I found myself brutally alone and facing a Goliath that sought to utterly destroy every fragment of God's peace and purpose in our lives. Alone with three young children aged eleven, seven and two, and with the shadow of satanic giants leering over our lives, I had to find within me the character of a giant killer.

"BROKENNESS AND FAILURE MAKE GREAT FERTILISER FOR TOMORROW'S SUCCESS."[52]

Giant killers are forged in hard times.

"Then said Achish unto his servants, Lo ye see this man is mad: wherefore then have ye brought him to me? Have I need of mad men, that ye have brought this fellow to play the mad man in my presence? shall this fellow come into my house?" 2 Samuel 21:14-15

Even David, the great giant killer who championed Israel, experienced times of massive self-doubt as he fled in fear of his life from godless King Saul. Fear, and the sense that his dream and all he lived for, were crumbling about him, filled his soul. Now he reached the lowest place of loneliness, exile and despair that he had ever known as he stumbled to Gath, the home of his mortal enemies.

With spittle dribbling down his beard, "feigning himself to be mad", he "scrabbled on the gate" of the palace of Achish the King of Gath. The giant killer had lost everything, even his trust of God and struggled in the pits of emotional despair. Now unbelievably, David was in Gath, the city he had terrorized when slayed its champion. It is incredible to me that, at the lowest time of his life, men searched him out to lead them. In fact, as he feigned madness in Gath, an army was on its way to him. In the next chapter, we look at this incredible time in David's life – the rise of his giant killing mighty men.

So low was David's emotional state here that the king of Gath tossed him aside and said:

> *"Have I need of mad men that ye have brought this fellow to play the mad man in my presence?..."[53]*

David's mind must have been assaulted by a tirade of questions.

- Where would he go?
- What would he do?
- Where was God?
- Where was his dream?
- Where was the awesome excitement that had filled him as the throngs of Israel had chanted his name?

He found himself in a lonely cave and struggled to find answers in his tortured mind.

Have you ever found yourself in that dreadful place of isolation, burnt out and wondering how things got to this situation? I know I have.

It seems that most of the greats of Scripture at some stage knew this dreadful place. Elijah, after stunning victories, sat totally depressed and wanted to die. The great prophet of fire was reduced to a broken emotional state. Here David was reduced to acting as a madman. Paul sat on death row and knew that all of Asia had left him. John the Baptist sat in a prison cell and wondered if his call had been correct. Timothy began to fold in fear at Ephesus only to be nursed back by Paul's second epistle.

"Times of general calamity and confusion have ever been productive of the greatest minds, the purest ore is produced from the hottest furnace and the brightest thunderbolt is the one elicited from the darkest storm."[54]

---

53   I Samuel 21:15
54   Caleb Colton pg 61

David the giant killer faced an onslaught from Hell that brought him to the end of himself.

Often it's not until we come to this place that we set ourselves to seek God and to rise up in His triumph.

It is most likely that the words of Psalm 142:14 were written by David in the cave of Adullam.

> *"I looked on my right hand, and beheld, but there was no man that would know me: refuge failed me; no man cared for my soul."* Psalm 142:4

Here was David: friendless, with no place to live and with a deep sense that no one cared. Yet, amazingly from here, David is about to step into his place of position, wealth, family, and friends. Often, just prior to stages of greatest influence, people experience times when everything that seems so vital is taken away and the man or woman find that all they really have is their relationship with God.

It is my testimony, that our impact into the nations took place during the most devastating time of my life. Let me share the story with you. The year of 1989 contained the lowest valleys yet amazing mountain tops. I was invited to conduct a miracle crusade in the beautiful city of Guadalcanal in the Solomon Islands.

As our plane circled the azure blue, green waters of Savo Bay, I was unaware of the intensity of the battle that had occurred in these waters in World War II. Dozens of warships, Japanese, American and Australian, lay in this undersea graveyard that came to be called Iron Bottom Sound.

In all, 55 capital ships were blasted to the sea bed in some of the deadliest sea battles in history. Japanese and American ships had fought in such close proximity that often they were firing on their own vessels.

In this distant tropical paradise, so seemingly insignificant to Japan and the USA, a battle had raged in 1942 that along with Midway, would determine the control of the South Pacific.

Over 25,000 young Japanese soldiers died on land, most from

starvation and disease. They called it "the hungry island". Over 3,000 American Marines died during brutal battles. On the first night battle General Achikis' Battallion was wiped out (over 1,200 men) as they charged in wave after wave against American Marines.

For months, the future of the Pacific Region, including my nation of Australia, hung in delicate balance as American marines and thousands of warriors of the Imperial Japanese army fought uncompromisingly for control of an island and an airstrip that would establish aerial dominance in this theatre of the Pacific War.

Back in Adelaide, I was personally in a seesaw battle for my own future as a preacher, father and husband. So intense was my struggle that I had lived in intense prayer and fasting for several months. It seemed that a conflict, beyond my control, raged all about me. I felt something of the emotions felt by David while he hid out in the cave of Adullam.

I had just completed four to five hours of prayer per day. I found myself in most ardent, earnest, heaven-storming, violently intense prayer. It was a prayer that rose out of some deep place within me that only tragic and desperate circumstances could find.

I firmly believe that resurrections come out of deaths and giant killers often rise out of tragedy.

The passion to "seize" God, to assault Heaven's gates, not with mild, passive token prayer, but with gut-wrenching reality, became the all-encompassing purpose of my existence.

As we landed on the very airstrip that was contested for so viciously all those years ago, I could sense a strange awareness of conquest and a surreal sacredness of this ground. Walking out of the airport, I was confronted by monuments erected to the marines who had fought so valiantly here. I could almost hear the bugle sounds and the shouts of men in the fury of battle; the muffled sounds of "banzai" charges of young Japanese men, at the prime of life, rushing headlong into a blanket of machine gun and rifle fire.

I did not realize that here, in this island paradise, my tormented and troubled life would be transformed. Guadalcanal is still littered with crashed airplanes, scores of sunken ships and bleached bones of the unburied dead. In this theatre of battle, 29,000 young Japanese men, 3,000 gallant American servicemen and thousands of seamen and airmen, had died violent deaths so far from their homes. For me, Guadalcanal became an amazing encounter with God's great global harvest.

This quiet and beautiful town of Honiara had seen war's fury. At Alligator River, 1,200 men of General Achiki's battalion had been mowed down in the first night of battle. The battles at Mantanikau River and Bloody Ridge are etched into the pages of military history. Fierce fighting, often hand to hand, raged here over many months. Battles on this island are now etched in history. Edson's raiders at Bloody Ridge displayed courage and coolness during a night of relentless banzai charges that inspires and astounds.

I was unaware that for months, another battle had been raging here in Guadalcanal. Every morning at 6:00 AM, hundreds of Christians met in the high places of the beautiful hills overlooking the town of Honiara and the magnificent Savo Bay. Their cry had echoed across the town, but more powerfully into the heart of God.

It is God's great delight to use people in difficult, even broken, circumstances, to bring all glory to Him. On arrival at Honiara, I was far from ready to preach. I had made a number of attempts to find a replacement. I was dejected, disappointed, broken, confused, failing of strength and wanting to hide out and "lick my wounds". My family in Australia was in tatters.

Yet these scriptures kept coming:

> "…out of weakness were made strong, waxed valiant in fight, turned to fight the armies of the aliens."
> Hebrews 11:34

> "…let the weak say I am strong." Joel 3:10

> "…the people that do know their God shall be strong, and do exploits." Daniel 11:32b

TIM HALL

The lights of the stadium lit the sky with a strange blue glow. The tropical air was filled with the sound of insects as we drove into God's arena. I had learned that day, that the stadium was built on a site that had seen intense fighting and death during the campaigns of World War II. Blood had been spilled on a massive scale for the redemption of this place. How could I preach to the mass crowds, with Hell seemingly unleashed on me?

I had to cross the river in full flood, armed with the weapons of God's armoury. I kept thinking of words by the great Holy Ghost gladiator, Reinhard Bonnke,

"Christians are not the hunted but the hunters."

The first day I tried to push in and pray. My mind darted and flashed with pictures and thoughts. I couldn't focus on the task as I desperately tried to push back the depression and the giant of despair that leered over me. But late in the afternoon, I began to feel around me the tangible sense of God's nearness.

As our team drove towards the stadium, we passed so many beautiful people, many with families, who carried mats and rugs. The air was balmy and filled with the sound of excitement and expectation. Suddenly, I was engulfed with a shockwave of holy awe, a sense that God was bigger than my emotional and family challenges. He was about to do something historical, something of His great purpose and plan.

This was the battle side of the overflowed river.[55] The crowd was only a few thousand on the first night but, as I began to preach, I felt waves of authority and power and God began a powerful work.

The following day, I fought again with the giant of depression throughout the day. But as we drove to the stadium, God again engulfed me with His overwhelming power. The crowd had doubled, and signs and miracles broke out wonderfully. Inspired and thrilled, I prophetically told people, "Tomorrow the glory of God will come in an unspeakable way."

The third day was an emotional struggle, yet a huge awareness of

---

55   Joshua 3

184

destiny was filling me. Could this be the birth of my deepest desires in God? Could this be the start of an onslaught into the nations? Why would something awesome be born in the time of personal tragedy? Certainly, the waves overwhelmed me. I was reminded of David's words:

> *"...all thy waves and thy billows are gone over me. Yet the Lord will command his lovingkindness in the daytime, and in the night his song shall be with me,..."*
> Psalm 42:7-8

The stadium filled and the atmosphere was electric with passionate anticipation. I preached from I John 3:8,

> *"For this purpose the Son of God was manifested, that he might destroy the works of the devil."*

It was an utterly prophetic word. As undeniable miracles broke out all night, I recall some deaf people testified to the healing, when suddenly, at the other end of the platform, a massive commotion erupted.

A man was carried to the meeting and laid on a mat at the end of the platform. He was totally paralysed, unable to speak and in this state for a long period of time. He stood with his arms raised in a gesture of worship, as he came onto the platform and held his mat bed aloft.

Throughout the stadium, faith rose in great waves. This released hundreds of people to seize their miracle. Waves of glory filled the city as result of this night. People came from other islands by boat, the markers buzzed with excited discussion of the awesome and unexpected things that were witnessed at the stadium each night. People streamed down from the hills as the word was "noised abroad". God had taken the field.

On the final night, the stadium was full of eager, fired-up, Solomon Islanders. A shell-shocked, battle-weary preacher was astonished and thousands of people were ushered supernaturally into the Kingdom of God.

The following day, I sat with the Prime Minister who presented me with a nice gift of appreciation and explained that this was the largest gathering since independence and expressed an open door to his nation. At the hotel, I sobbed at the sheer goodness and greatness of our awesome God, who shows himself so mighty in our darkest hours of challenge.

My friend, cross your river, though it may be flooding at the banks. Take up the whole armour of God, shield of faith, the mighty instruments of our warfare and cross into your destiny.

Often circumstances seem impossible, everything opposes logic, yet we know that God is speaking "now is the time", "seize the opportunity". Giant killers do not look at the reasons why something can't be done. They move with God and His timing.

Cross the flooded river, forget the impossibilities, and watch God's incredible arm bared on your behalf.

David was at his lowest place emotionally and physically yet he was about to be launched into the greatest phase of his destiny.

DAVID'S MIGHTY MEN

GIANT KILLERS PRODUCE GIANT KILLERS

"David therefore departed thence, and escaped to the cave Adullam: and when his brethren and all his father's house heard it, they went down thither to him.

And every one that was in distress, and every one that was in debt, and every one that was discontented, gathered themselves unto him; and he became a captain over them: and there were with him about four hundred men." 1 Samuel 22:1-2

"These also are the chief of the mighty men whom David had, who strengthened themselves with him in his kingdom..." 1 Chronicles 11:10

Just as Moses mentored and raised up Joshua and Caleb, destroyers of giants, so David raised up under him a legendary and ferocious group of giant slayers known as his "mighty men". These men of renown completed the great task, commenced by Moses, Joshua, Caleb and David, of the eradication of the last remnant of giants from Gaza, Ashdod and Gath. Their rise from devastation to triumphant conqueror status is one of the Bible's mighty motivational stories.

A ragged, defeated group of men, crushed under the compromising, sin-soaked leadership of King Saul, staggered into David's cave of hiding, far from the stench of defeat that hung as a pall over invaded Israel. Philistine soldiers swarmed the streets of the cities of God. The bodies of King Saul and Jonathan hung on the walls of Bethshan as trophies of the success of the Philistine gods over the God of Israel. David was in great personal turmoil as he hid in the cave of Adullam.

The group of broken men came to him in economic debt, desperate to break these shackles. They came to him discontented, angry, chafed, heavy in heart and made bitter by life's circumstances. They came to him in distress, confined, boxed in, disabled and anguished. They came to him compressed, constrained and full of hurt. They came to this exiled man because they knew that in him flowed the pulse of God's kingdom-shaking anointing. They came to David because in him was the God-given steel that took him onto the lonely battlefield of Shochoh to face the most awesome warrior that had ever been seen by Israel's host. In him was the uncompromising zeal that caused him to charge fearlessly at the demonised giant to bring him down with a stone.

They gathered to David with the declaration, "we are thy bone and thy flesh"[56] Their hearts were in total covenant with the man they knew had been raised up by God in this sad hour of their nation's history.

These damaged and disillusioned men who came to join David

---

56   I Chronicles 11:1

became known as David's mighty men, a group of warriors of daring, ferocity, endurance and might unseen in Israel's history. They stand alone in Scripture for their raw, heroic exploits. They were seemingly unintimidated by any situation that confronted them.

The name mighty men comes from the Hebrew word *gibbor gibbor*[57], which means "powerful warrior, champion, excelling mighty man, valiant man, tyrant, giant and man of renown."

These men were forged from desperate brokenness to mighty heroes in a short time as they aligned themselves to David.

Surely the "mighty man" was resident within them waiting for a leader who could draw him out. In the book of Joel we read,

> "...*Prepare war, wake up the mighty men, let all the men of war draw near; let them come up*" Joel 3:9

The Hebrew word translated wake up is `*ur*[58] and means "open the eyes, stir up, raise up, waken from sleep". This is the challenge to every leader. Our role is, by the power of God, to cause ordinary people around us to rise up and awaken the sleeping mighty man within and to step out into a life of daring exploits for Jesus.

In these perilous days of fear, anxiety and total uncertainty, people are desperate for strong leadership. They are seeking out those who can give them guidance and self belief and who can help instil purpose and direction to their lives.

Shattered, disillusioned men sought out David because in him they had seen unbridled raw courage in the face of deadly opposition. In him they sensed destiny, God-given vision and a supernatural anointing from God. They sensed and somehow knew that David had a king's anointing with a passion for his nation that burned in his belly and the courage to bring victory into their decimated world. They came to David ready to totally commit their lives, their families and their destinies into his hand.

Shattered people, damaged by the cares and trials of life, are looking for us to rise up under the awesome and mighty anointing of the Holy <u>Ghost. They are</u> searching out leaders who are uncompromising,

57   Strong's H1368
58   Strong's H5782

courageous and exuding vision and purpose. They are ready to wholeheartedly follow men and women who know their God and have clear goals and a vision from Heaven. Giant killers are not wanting sickly, compromising programmes where the leaders are afraid to step out for fear of offending people. They are ready to follow the courageous leaders whose total purpose is to please the One who called them.

David's mighty men came to him ready for a total life transformation and truly, as written in Hebrews 11:34, "out of weakness were made strong (supernaturally empowered with divine ability)."

A GREAT MENTOR

I thank God for the mentor God gave me over 35 years ago. Living far from God, I had become very disillusioned with Satan's rule in my life.

When I came and gave my life to Christ, I was a wild young man, and lived very much as a true "alien" from the Kingdom of God. I lived for the moment with little real sense of responsibility.

Dr Andrew Evans, the Senior Pastor of Australia's largest Pentecostal church of the time, had received a word from God:

"As Paul had a Timothy to train, I am giving you a Timothy to shape into a man of God."

I walked into his church in 1974 with long hair and the stench of alcohol all over me. I was trained as an artist and only really lived to party and paint. I was set to live a short, wild existence. This night circumstances brought me into this great, thriving church. I settled in the back row and enjoyed the bright music – it felt good, even soothing. But the preacher brought a dramatic change. He preached with holy fire and power until I simply wanted to run. Finally, to my great relief, he stopped his message and began to invite people to come and find Christ. I knew that I desperately needed to surrender to the Lord but pride kept me standing unmoved like a statue. Suddenly, I felt a hand on my shoulder but I knew no-one was there – not anyone I could see. I began to rush towards the altar to find Christ. As I stood there I shook and trembled as God took over my being.

Dr Andrew Evans, until recently a Senator in the South Australian Government, heard the voice of the Lord, "That Timothy I have spoken about is down there." He fastened his eyes on me and must have thought, "Not possible."

As he stood in front of me, he quietly asked, "What is your name, son?"

"Tim," I answered.

Tears rolled down his face as he laid his hand on my head and asked God to mightily fill me with His power. I began to bellow out "the unutterable gushings of my soul".

When I first came to work for Dr Andrew Evans, I was always moved by his passion to win the lost. I saw in him a desire to build a great work for God and I knew he had been a successful and courageous missionary in Papua New Guinea. My total desire was to be "bone of his bone" and "flesh of his flesh" in serving God.

From that day, like David of old, my pastor took me under his wing. I travelled with him when he preached in different places and soon became his youth pastor. He encouraged and mentored me and has enjoyed every success we have experienced over 30 years.

This apostle of God has raised up two sons, who today have churches with thousands of members, and spiritual sons with large churches of similar size, as well as ministries like ours that have touched multitudes of people.

GODLY ALIGNMENT BRINGS PERSONAL ENLARGEMENT

In 1 Chronicles 11:10, we read that David's mighty men, "strengthened themselves with him in his kingdom". The Hebrew word chazaq[59] means "to fasten upon", "to strengthen". These men had fastened themselves to David in strong covenant. In this "bone

---

59   Strong's H2388

of bone" relationship, submitted to the vision and goals of this mighty man, they grew incredibly in stature, purpose and daring.

Shaka Zulu, the Alexander the Great of Southern Africa who raised up the mightiest army Africa has ever seen, said,

"To be a conqueror, be apprenticed to a conqueror."

We must seriously choose who can help us and speak into our lives.

As I have watched key men rise to great heights in Australia and around the world, almost all have been loyally submitted to a man of God of substance, vision and anointing. In due time, God launched them from that strong foundation to a place of great achievement in their own right.

At this point, let me ask you some probing questions:

- To whom are you aligned?
- Are you aligned and related to people who inspire and challenge you?
- Are those alliances causing you to grow in stature, maturity and impact?
- Are you raising up apprentices around you with a goal to see them far exceed your own achievements?
- Are you aligned with people around you who can speak into your life?
- Are you aligned to achievers constantly growing or people who just make you feel comfortable.
- Are you aligned to people who keep you accountable and can talk to you with bold honesty?

The impact of the next generation will be the final assessment of our achievements. Perhaps my greatest thrill in ministry is to watch our own son David grow rapidly in stature as pastor of our home church and minister in significant conferences, crusades and churches across the world. For years he has faithfully served our ministry and been "bone of our bone" and "flesh of our flesh" and now the world is opening to him incredibly in his late twenties.

The great Prophet Elijah raised up a prophet after him who produced double the number of miracles seen in his own ministry. Elijah's mantle came with double portion on Elisha and the great prophetic impact shook the nation. Elisha's awesome gifting saw the dead raised, great miracles and healing, provision and knowledge and yet tragically Elisha did not raise up an apprentice after him but took his mantle to the grave. We know this fact because a dead man, thrown into Elisha's tomb, touched his dead bones and was raised to life.[60] The mighty anointing was closed up in a grave. Elisha's gift went with him to the tomb. Who are you raising up to follow in your steps? What will be our legacy in coming generations?

DAVID'S APPRENTICES BECAME GIANT KILLERS

Day by day, broken, dejected, desperate men came to David to be restored in strength, hope and vision.

David's mighty men "strengthened themselves with him" in the cave of Adullam. The Hebrew word chazaq[61] also means, "to seize, courage, strength, fortification, to wax mighty, to be repaired, restored, to behave one's self valiantly". All of these characteristics arose in David's mighty men out of alliance with him. Out of weakness, defeat, despair, debt and total disillusionment, they became an unstoppable force of Spirit-empowered warriors of legendary renown.

I think the writer to the Hebrews (probably Paul) had David's mighty men in mind when he wrote:

> "Who through faith subdued kingdoms, wrought righteousness, obtained promises, stopped the mouths of lions, Quenched the violence of fire, escaped the edge of the sword, out of weakness were made strong, waxed valiant in fight, turned to flight the armies of the aliens."

60   2 Kings 13:21
61   Strong's H2388

Hebrews 11:33-34

These dejected and discouraged men grew from despair to triumph under the mighty anointing of David. The apprentices became champions. They truly, "waxed valiant in fight".[62] The Greek word for waxed is ginomai and means to be "formed, made or created from nothing"[63]. David's mighty men were "made, formed and created" from 400 rejects who sought hope in their shattered worlds. They went on to be unstoppable men of renown.

ENTER THE APPRENTICES

David began his great destiny on planet earth as a giant killer. His last great recorded battle in Scripture was against a Philistine army championed by four giants of Gath, brothers of Goliath. This time David was surrounded by his valiant men who had already killed giants with David and they eradicated the last of these intimidating warriors.

> *"Moreover the Philistines had yet war again with Israel; and David went down, and his servants with him, and fought against the Philistines: and David waxed faint.*
>
> *And Ishbibenob, which was of the sons of the giant, the weight of whose spear weighed three hundred shekels of brass in weight, he being girded with a new sword, thought to have slain David.*
>
> *But Abishai the son of Zeruiah succoured him, and smote the Philistine, and killed him. Then the men of David sware unto him, saying, Thou shalt go no more out with us to battle, that thou quench not the light of Israel.*
>
> *And it came to pass after this, that there was again a battle with the Philistines at Gob: then Sibbechai the*

---

62   Hebrews 11:34
63   Key Word Study Bible, Lexical aids to New Testament page 1700

Hushathite slew Saph, which was of the sons of the giant.

And there was again a battle in Gob with the Philistines, where Elhanan the son of Jaareoregim, a Bethlehemite, slew the brother of Goliath the Gittite, the staff of whose spear was like a weaver's beam.

And there was yet a battle in Gath, where was a man of great stature, that had on every hand six fingers, and on every foot six toes, four and twenty in number; and he also was born to the giant.

And when he defied Israel, Jonathan the son of Shimea the brother of David slew him.

These four were born to the giant in Gath, and fell by the hand of David, and by the hand of his servants."
2 Samuel 21:15-22

WHEN GODLINESS IS REMOVED, GIANTS BREED

The first of the giants that David and his mighty men confronted was Ishbibenob, one of the sons of the giant (of Gath). He was one of Goliath's brothers or, as some believe, one of Goliath's sons. The name Ishbibenob is interesting. It simply means, "an inhabitant of Nob". Nob was an interesting place. It was here that the sword of Goliath had been kept by the priest Ahimelech until David, pursued by Saul, came to collect it (1 Samuel 21:8-9). Here at Nob, Saul committed one of the most heinous crimes in Scripture. Saul, totally incensed and desperate to track down and kill David, came to Nob to inquire of Ahimelech as to the help given to his escaping "enemy".

Ahimelech's plea to Saul of David's faithfulness fell on deaf ears. His instruction to Doeg the Edomite saw 85 ephod-wearing priests brutally murdered. Little wonder that in the years ahead, a brutal giant with a terrible resolve and a new sword rose up against God's people out of this very place.

As we have watched prayer taken out of the American school system and Christian values dismantled in the Western world, we see great giants rising with new honed swords to fight with a new resolve and savage purpose.

This "inhabitant of Nob" came against David girded with a new sword. A new weapon was forged against David. A new giant, with a new weapon was raised up in the place where Goliath's sword had been kept for a season.

This new giant armed with his new weapon came onto the field of battle seeking out the old foe, David. David was old and should have retired but he too had a new weapon, honed and sharpened equipped moulded and trained at his side, a young fearless warrior called Abishai. His name means "gift of my father". The giant came ferociously at the old warrior David, who was weakened and tired. But David's new weapon Abishai rushed out and strengthened David before he cut down Isbibenob in his tracks. Abishai was God's gift to David. He was now trained up to stand with, strengthen and defend him and to become the new generation of giant killers.

YOUR INHERITANCE

Those people who come to you to be mentored and trained are an awesome gift of the Father. They are your inheritance. They are the most wonderful statement of God's confidence in you. God's promise to us is that our "seed shall be mighty upon earth".[64]

As we study these mighty men of David we firstly see them come to him as men who faced their own leering giants: devastated, disillusioned and shattered by Saul's total failure. Later, we see a group of men who are mirror images of David do the same heroic acts, supremely confident in their skill and God-given anointing. Each of the giants faced by Abishai, Sibbechai, Elhanan and Jonathan (David's nephew) were slain with ease. The names of these other giant killers I found interesting, Elhanan means "gracious" and Jonathan means "Jehovah given". Certainly these mighty men were God's gracious gifts to David. What joy they must have brought to the heart of the old giant killer.

People are still seeking out giant killers to follow, to be mentored by and to fashion themselves after. Giant killers set the pattern and open the path. They are God's ice-breakers in the Kingdom.

David's enormous victory over Goliath, unquestioned courage, God-breathed vision and obvious anointing of kingly dominion, caused men of war, valiant men and men of resolve to seek him out.

The same qualities attract the valiant, qualified, gifted, anointed people of vision today. Like insects to a light, valiant Kingdom men and women will seek out their anointed, unintimidated giant killer. People who are struggling with debt, dejected by life's dealings and crushed by injustice are seeking out God's warriors. God will direct them to the place where they can be forged and shaped as future giant killers.

It is interesting that they came together to Hebron (formerly Kirjath-Arba) where Caleb had shattered the four controlling giants of that region. It was the perfect place for a giant killer to receive his kingly coronation, a place made sacred by a man of military renown – Caleb.

We are told that people kept coming to David day after day until they were like the great "host of God"[65]. They came from all over Israel, defeated people ready to be transformed.

There are business people, I.T. specialists, entrepreneurs, sporting stars and people extraordinary in their fields, that are desperate to align themselves with Christian leaders. They can enter into a covenant that will see them, not only totally enhance the church or ministry, but allow them to grow to great heights in their own gifting.

I have a friend in the USA whose powerful church has attracted a large number of Navy Seals. This pastor must be presenting a strong, manly gospel if these elite men of the US Forces choose to make his church their home. Pastor Ray McCauley in South Africa is a pastor to many of the nation's elite sportsmen. The former champion body builder presents a vision and gospel in the great Randburg Rhema Church that has seen it become a comfortable spiritual home for these people. As leaders, we must prepare a place for people where they feel confident, secure and certain regarding the fulfilment of their dreams.

Significant men and women are preparing their hearts and lives for great achievement but are cautiously waiting for the man or woman with whom they are to join themselves "bone of bone" and "flesh of flesh". Here pastors need to ask these questions:

---

65   I Chronicles 12:22

1. Am I leading with conviction and purpose that will cause people to whole heartedly commit to our vision?
2. Is my passion to raise people up so that they can fulfil their destinies?
3. Do I want those around me to so develop under my leadership that they will ultimately surpass me?
4. Do I carry an anointing of strength, a clear vision and courage of conviction, which will cause God's choice, called warriors to join me?
5. What sort of people are being attracted to my leadership?
6. Ten years from now, how many of those trusted to my care will be doing great exploits?

THE SATISFACTION OF MINISTRY

Recently, I attended a major youth conference in Australia. Thousands of young people had come from around the world and were filled with a holy enthusiasm and passion. I had been through a time of personal soul-searching, wondering what had remained after 30 years of conferences and crusades across the earth.

Sitting in the green room after the meeting, one after the other, the young leaders, who are all on fire for God, came to me.

"Did you know that I was set ablaze for Jesus in one of your meetings ten years ago?" asked one young man.

"I was first touched by God and called to ministry in one of your meetings," said a young man pioneering a powerful church in the USA.

Another, who now oversees the youth of another State, declared, "If you hadn't taken me under your wing and believed in me, I would not have made it for God."

Today, he is the associate minister in a major church and is travelling globally as well as overseeing thousands of young people in his State. That night I realised that I had been used of God to impact and inspire in some way every leader in that green room.

I returned home that night with a great sense of God saying to me, "These are your gifts and rewards. Here is your satisfaction in ministry".

Several days ago, I flew to Melbourne, Australia to visit a critically ill friend. God gave me the privilege years ago of leading both he and his wife to Christ. This was followed shortly after by his sons. God put it in my heart to build my life and ministry gifts into this family. This couple went on to pioneer and build strong churches in Queensland, the ACT (Australian Capital Territory) and Victoria, while their eldest son has pastored large churches, went to Africa pioneering and today has a large church in England.

Lying critically ill on his bed a few days ago, he looked me in the eye and said, "I want to thank you. Because of you, my whole family is saved, including grandchildren, and we have touched multiple thousands of people in churches and mass crusades in Papua New Guinea."

I thought, "Here is the satisfaction of ministry. This makes all the pain, pressure, rejection and misunderstanding that I have felt fade away to nothing."

One of the finest children's ministers in Australia spoke to me recently. He is pastoring one of the largest children's works in Australia and establishing world class resources for hundreds of children's works.

He shared with me how some years ago he was totally disillusioned and ready to walk away from anything to do with God. He decided to come to one of my meetings with the certainty within that if nothing happened that night, he would walk away. He sat and waited. Nothing happened.

After a long night of ministry, altar calls and laying on of hands and prophecy, the meeting was closed.

As I was leaving the church building, my eyes fell on this young man and the Spirit of the Lord quickened within me.

I called him, not realising that he was walking away from God.

He told me that, on that night, I had prophesied the disappointment that he felt but declared to him that God was forming within him a mighty gift that would impact multitudes of children and that he would be significant in God's purposes. His life was touched by the mighty power of God and in that instant, his destiny changed.

From discouragement, disappointment and despair, God has raised him up, touching multitudes of children.

DAVID'S MIGHTY MEN BECAME GIANT KILLERS BY JOINING THEMSELVES TO ONE

These men were transformed by simply being around the great giant killer. These men began to do extraordinary exploits. Adino, Eleazar and Shammah rose to prominence as they faced overwhelming odds, were faithful in most humble situations and by incredible perseverance. Adino lifted his spear against 800 men, whom he slew at one time. Eleazar fought alongside David until, "his hand clave to the sword",[66] while Shammah fought relentlessly to protect a vegetable garden.

It is said in the sporting arena that there are those on the field who cause others around them to stand tall. This indeed speaks of David.

A generation of giant killers rose up around David who seemed invincible, men like Abishai and Benaiah who stood up against a 2.7 m (9 foot) Egyptian giant with a spear like a weaver's beam. Benaiah carried a staff only but snatched the spear out of the giant's hand and drove it through his body.

I am convinced that the greatest satisfaction we can ever have as Christians will be to look back on the giant killing generation we have mentored and raised up behind us and to watch them stepping up on the foundation we have laid to do exploits far beyond those that we have achieved.

CHARACTERISTICS OF A MIGHTY MAN

In previous chapters we have looked at the characteristics of the giant killers. In the twelfth chapter of 1 Chronicles, we find the character traits of David's mighty men. We need to look at these and consider how we can incorporate them into our lives and ministries.

---

66   2 Samuel 23:10

1. THEY WERE ALL "MIGHTY MEN OF VALOUR"

We have already seen that David took these broken, disillusioned men and forged them into elite warriors of renown. In 1 Chronicles we find that they were all mighty men.

> *"And of the Gadites there separated themselves unto David into the hold to the wilderness men of might, and men of war fit for the battle, that could handle shield and buckler, whose faces were like the faces of lions, and were as swift as the roes upon the mountains."*
> 1 Chronicles 12:8

> *"And they helped David against the band of the rovers: for they were all mighty men of valour, and were captains in the host."* 1 Chronicles 12:21

> *"Of the children of Simeon, mighty men of valour for the war, seven thousand and one hundred"*
> 1 Chronicles 12:25

In verse 8 we read that they were men of "might" (strength, power, ability, valiant in battle, virtuous, strong)[67] and men of military campaign, strong and able to keep rank. It is interesting that the Hebrew word for war (tsaba)[68] can also be translated as worship. No doubt, David's mighty men had learnt from their mentor the awesome place of worship in the life of a giant killer.

In the book of Zechariah 12:8, we see that in the last days the inhabitants of Jerusalem will mount up with great strength:

> *"...and he that is feeble among them at that day shall be as David; and the house of David shall be as God, as the angel of the LORD before them."*

---

67   Strong's H2428
68   Strong's H6635

I take this as a prophetic word also for the end time Church. It is truly time for the Body of Christ to be known individually and collectively as Jesus' mighty men and women.

This great end time spiritual conflict will be characterised by mighty acts of audacious valour as the Body of Christ turns from greed and self gratification to a passionate force of warriors plundering the Gates of Hell.

People of valour will have to rise out of the comfort and security of church sheepfolds to reach the greatest harvest ever in human history.

2. DAVID'S MIGHTY MEN WERE PEOPLE WITH GREAT PURPOSE

Even when life had seemingly been so crushing with Saul's defeat and the Philistine invasion, a powerful sense of purpose remained deeply set in the hearts of these mighty men. The fact that, even in crushing defeat, a powerful hope and sense of purpose remained within tells us that here were men that could be shaped, built and trained for greatness.

They sought out David and came to him with strong resolve.

> "...came to David to Hebron, to turn the kingdom of Saul to him..." 1 Chronicles 12:23

Their own introduction to David is filled with purpose, "Behold, we are thy bone and thy flesh."[69] The Message Bible puts 1 Chronicles 11:1 this way:

> "Look at us...We're your very flesh and blood."

They came with a mighty passion and purpose to see their nation saved.

They came from a defeated kingdom to see a new kingdom set in place of triumph and victory.

---

69   1 Chronicles 11:1

Jesus didn't come to start a new religion. He came to usher in the Kingdom of God.

Giant killers are intent on ushering in a kingdom, God's mighty Kingdom. David's defeat of Goliath was the catalyst that ushered in a new kingdom. This has to be our passion.

Giant killers are people of intense purpose, totally committed to bringing the Kingdom of God into the midst of a devastated generation.

When David argued with his brother Eliab, he asked the great question:

"Is there not a cause?"[70]

David's mighty men asked the same question: they sought out David as leader knowing him to be God's man of cause and purpose.

We need to ask ourselves certain questions at this point.

1. Are we full of single-minded purpose?
2. Are we consumed with a passion to fulfil our God-given destiny?
3. Do we wake up with purpose and passion to act?

Giant killers must be people of white hot, clear cut purpose.

3. THEY WERE "EXPERT IN WAR, WITH ALL INSTRUMENTS OF WAR"[71]

"Of Zebulun, such as went forth to battle, expert in war, with all instruments of war,... which could keep rank: they were not of double heart." 1 Chronicles 12:33

In 1 Chronicles 12, we read that the mighty men were armed (verse 2) and were ambidextrous in the use of weapons. We are told that they were men of strategies in battle, fully armed (verses 8, 23, 33, 37) with all the instruments of battle.

---

70   1 Samuel 17:29
71   1 Chronicles 12:33

1. They were expert in war. They had honed their skills in battle through intense, disciplined training. They must have studied military strategy and method and drawn their understanding from past victories and defeats of the armies that had gone before. It is said of Napoleon that his detailed planning of battles was so precise that he had lived out every move in minute detail before one shot was fired.

2. They had all the instruments of war. Not only were they skilled and trained in battle techniques but they had also built and developed instruments for all aspects of war.

   This is our challenge, as God's 21st Century mighty men, to be honed in the Word of God and the spiritual gifts to the highest level possible. It is also time to make use of every piece of technology and computer software that will enhance everything we wish to achieve in gathering our portion of the great end time harvest.

3. They could keep rank. They moved together as a tight, well-disciplined unit, with every man clear in his role. They knew their objectives and moved together with united purpose. The strength of the famous legions of Rome was their extraordinary discipline and their great ability to keep rank and move as a single unit regardless of opposition or terrain.

   Every year I preach in an outstanding church in Bloemfontein. The pastor at Boshoff was a military man, as were most of his team. The church has a military sense of purpose and precision in everything they do. There is a strong sense of discipline and chain of command all developed in a real sense of love, respect and passion for the lost. Vision is clearly spelt out and presented as a battle plan. It has the sense of an anointed military unit. Every year it grows by around 2,000 or more in number. There are currently over 28,000 members.

4. They were not of double heart. They were fully armed.

David's mighty men had honed their military skills. In 1 Chronicles 12:2 we read:

> *"They were armed with bows, and could use both the right hand and the left in hurling stones and shooting arrows out of a bow, even of Saul's brethren of Benjamin."*

These men could use both right hand and left with slings and bows. To gain some real understanding of the accuracy of the Benjaminite slinger, we need to consider the description in Judges 20:16:

> *"Among all this people there were seven hundred chosen men lefthanded; every one could sling stones at an hair breadth, and not miss."*

Incredible! Imagine being able to sling a stone so accurately, at "an hair's breadth", and not miss. It seems they could hurl accurately over 200 yards. Amazingly, these of David's mighty men[72] could do this with right and left hand. David's mighty men were "experts in war" trained, tried and honed.

From the time of my salvation, I have felt an extraordinary passion to be honed for battle. I have been frustrated by the disparity that seemed to exist between the first century church and the Body of Christ that I have seen, where miracles and the mighty demonstration of God are the exception rather than the rule.

David told us that God was training and strengthening his hands for battle.

> *"He teacheth my hands to war; so that a bow of steel is broken by mine arms."* 2 Samuel 22:35

As a young man stepping out in ministry, I read much of John G. Lake, the mighty man of God used mightily in South Africa. As a result, I continually asked God to make my hands weapons that carried the <u>lightning fire of</u> God to terrify the arch enemy of men's souls. I went

72   1 Chronicles 12:2

alone into the mountains for weeks at a time and passionately desired to be a honed weapon of God, "a sharp threshing instrument having teeth" that God could use to "thresh the mountains"[73]. My early forays into the realm of the miraculous were nerve-wracking and not always fruitful. Only as I stepped out in prayer and action that the gifts that now touch multitudes of people were honed and developed.

EQUIPPED WITH ALL THE WEAPONS

I had finished preaching and ministering in a New Zealand church several decades ago. I was an enthusiastic, hungry young man who was always desperate to see the demonstrated power of God. This characteristic in my life has never changed. This gospel of the Kingdom is a demonstrated gospel, a gospel of signs, wonders and mighty miracles. The thing that sets Christianity apart from other religions is the brooding power of the Holy Spirit, "confirming the word with signs that follow."[74]

I was sitting in an armchair at the pastor's home that night, feeling of all men "most miserable". The small crowd had been less responsive than the pot plants on the platform. It seemed like the sick had dared me, this young evangelist upstart, to even try to heal them. The normal flow of the word of knowledge had been bland and no-one had found Christ. Only one positive thing had happened. One man had come with major back problems caused by a rugby injury. This great game, epidemic in proportion in New Zealand, will always keep active any healing evangelist who goes there to minister.

I had a clear word of knowledge about his condition and the power of God was unleashed on him.

As I laid hands on him, he shot backwards through several rows of seats and finished in an ungainly position, totally healed. He was ecstatic, and jumped about like he had just eaten a handful of jumping beans.

Back at the pastor's home, I sat in the armchair thinking about

---

73   Isaiah 41:15
74   Mark 16:20

the deadness of the night. We began to laugh and rejoice hysterically over the one positive influence: this one healing and the man's total infectious enthusiasm.

Here is a great key to any preacher. Never go home from any meeting thinking about what didn't happen. Don't dwell on the things that should have happened but set your eyes clearly on the positive even if it's just one small thing. One evangelist preached his heart out one night in the USA and only one young boy came down to be saved – Billy Graham.

If a meeting seems like a total failure, think of past successes and future victories. Don't beat yourself up and analyse and torment yourself. Read a few chapters from the Book of Acts or from John G. Lake or Smith Wigglesworth. Don't let the giants of doubt or the negative attitudes of people or a lack of responsiveness bring you down. Just take hold of God with real purpose. Sometimes as a young man just before preaching, I would come under a great sense of emptiness and fear that nothing would happen in that meeting. A voice would say, "You are alone. Nothing is going to happen with these people." I learnt to simply tell this giant, "Get out of my road. Tonight this place will break open with the glory of God, this will be a powerful and unforgettable move of the God who is in me, over me, through me and who is going to do 'exceedingly abundantly beyond anything I can ask or think according to His mighty power that is working within me.'[75] "

The next morning, I was awakened with a phone call at an hour that is not popular for evangelists who have preached long and stayed up with the pastor talking for hours. It was Mr "Jumping Beans".

"I'm totally healed, totally healed. I'm so excited," he explained.

Endeavouring to give the impression of one who had been up since before sunrise dissecting the Greek and Hebrew scriptures, I cleared my croaky throat with some well-placed "Hallelujahs", "praise Gods" and a selection of well-chosen and enthusiastic Pentecostal phrases of excited bliss.

This genuine excitement that I was enjoying, despite the fact that the rooster outside still hadn't crowed, was very instantly extinguished

---

by his next piece of information.

"I phoned my friend last night and told him you will come over at 10 o'clock this morning and raise him up."

"What is his problem?" I asked, feeling a little anxious.

"Well," said Brother "Jumping Beans", "Firstly, he's not a believer, knows nothing about the Bible and some years ago was crushed against a wall by a truck, smashing his spine but I told him you will come over and raise him up."

Terror gripped me, as I was just beginning my journey into the arena of the miraculous of God. This was a serious injury.

"What is his condition then?" I asked. The reply sent flying whatever sense of faith I was endeavouring to muster.

"Well, he is bent double and faces the ground. He is constantly on pain killing injections and his spine is so out of alignment that one leg is around 7.6 cm (3 inches) shorter than the other."

"And I'm coming to heal him at 10 o'clock," I thought.

I laboured over every mouthful of cornflakes at breakfast. I'll tell you honestly, I just wanted to run. God seemed to have taken a vacation and I was feeling totally spiritually impotent. The sound of the doorbell seemed to usher me with executioners on the green mile walk. I had put on a bright preacher's tie, made sure I had some breath freshener and tried to get my hair in perfect place like an American "tele-evangelist" but I was inwardly greatly afraid.

Looking back, the car ride to the house was amusing. Brother "Jumping Beans" was in orbit, in raptures of expectation. The preacher, in total despair, was trying to look and sound like "God's man of faith and power" while inwardly feeling like "God's man of paste and flour". What would I do? Where would I start?

Standing at the door, clutching my Bible, I watched Brother "J.B." press the bell. The noise brought shuddering reality to my already terrified state. The sound of his wife's footsteps was even worse.

"He is in tremendous pain," she said.

Ushering us into the lounge room, she went to bring her crippled husband to the room. I wasn't looking at Brother "J.B." I was afraid my eyes would show my grasshopper state before this giant that was coming to taunt me. But at least I had taken the field.

My friend, that is the first step. Put yourself in the place where miracles occur. Remember courage is not the absence of fear. It is the mastery of it.

As the man was ushered into the room in agonizing pain, his wife slowly eased him into his pillowed, prepared chair. His face was contorted with pain as he grimaced.

"What should I say?" I thought.

I began gingerly, "I'm not the healer sir – Jesus is." This is the greatest cop-out that the Church has made for years. In His name, by our hands, we are God's healers on the earth.

Jesus did not say, ask me to heal the sick. He commissioned us and equipped us with His supernatural weaponry to go and heal everywhere. He has armed us with all the weapons of His warfare. He has put at our disposal all the instruments of war.

I did learn one huge lesson that morning.

I said, "Sir, let me tell you what God has said in His word."

Without looking at him, I began to share the Scriptures on healing that I had been memorising and speaking continually.

> *"So shall my word be that goeth forth out of my mouth: it shall not return unto me void, but it shall accomplish that which I please, and it shall prosper in the thing whereto I sent it."* Isaiah 55:11

- The Word does not return void.
- The Word shall accomplish.
- The Word shall prosper.

The Scriptures seemed to gain momentum and I became very aware of the presence of the God who broods over His "word to perform it".[76]

How can you describe faith? Isn't it amazing how this eternal Word can stir this invisible, yet tangible, "substance" called faith[77]?

---

76   Jeremiah 1:12
77   Hebrews 11:1

I looked up and caught the man's eyes. It was the first time I had looked into his face. His eyes were alive with freshly God-breathed faith. In my heart, I knew we stood on the threshold of a real miracle, a mighty creative, restoring demonstration of power.

Suddenly I felt that my hands were truly weapons and that my words were filled with devil-terrifying authority.

Taking him by the hands, I commanded, "Stand up on your feet".

He struggled half way but with a second volley of authority, "Stand up straight," his spine gave a loud crack and he was standing straight with tears flowing down his face.

He was dramatically saved, along with his whole family, that morning. The meetings at that church went from a small cynical group, to a packed house of faith-filled hungry people seeking the touch of God's divine hand. This is the result I read in the Book of Acts, as reports of mighty miracles filled the cities. Whole populations rushed out to see the works of God. People haven't changed and the results of the miraculous still draw the multitudes.

God is wanting our churches to echo with the reports of a living, active God moving in the midst. It is God's great desire that we, like David's mighty men, have all the instruments of war.

Since that day, we have enjoyed watching the most extraordinary demonstrations of God's power in many nations.

Recently, I sat with a man who had worked with the great preacher, A. A. Allen.

During the great season of miraculous demonstration that swept America during the 1950s and 1960s, A.A. Allen was one of the people most significantly used by God. In his great tent meetings, tens of thousands of people came to see and experience the extraordinary release of God's mighty power. Crippled bodies, paralysed limbs, cancers and tumours all gave way to the mighty gifting upon Allen's life.

This man, who had worked alongside the greatly gifted man of God, described remarkable creative miracles where eyes formed in the sockets of a young child. He talked of nights when rows of wheelchairs were emptied.

He explained to me that, at the commencement of A.A. Allen's ministry, he was frustrated as to how he could lay hands on all the multitudes in the largest of his meetings. As he enquired of God, the Lord said, "Do what Peter did. Use your shadow."[78]

A large, strong light was set up behind him on the platform and moved about casting a shadow over the crowd. As the light was turned on and the shadow moved over the masses, mighty miracles exploded out on every side. In this way, he learned to minister on a mass scale.

The man went on to tell me how Allen was working at his headquarters and had to walk out through his TV studio. Many of his staff were involved in a variety of tasks in this area. For some reason, a large light was illuminated in one section of the studio. As Allen quietly walked through, his shadow passed over the workers who were suddenly overcome by the power of God, fell over, were healed and shaken as the great man's shadow passed over them.

Several months ago, I was ministering in New South Wales, Australia. A five-year-old boy suffering from autism was brought to our meeting for prayer.

Autism is a sickness that terribly hinders a child's mental and physical development and robs him emotionally and socially.

This young boy's condition had so affected his father's faith that he had totally backslidden from Christ. His mother had never found Jesus as her Saviour.

A family friend brought the boy for prayer. As I laid hands on him, the power of God pulsed through him. He lay on the floor with the evident sense that something mighty was taking place in him.

When he was returned to his home that night, a wonderful thing took place. His mother had bought him a puppy, hoping that it might help to unlock his paralysed emotions. On seeing the pup, he ran with an outpouring of excitement and displayed feelings and emotions that his mother had never seen before. She immediately began to weep, knowing that a significant miracle had occurred. He then told her how he had seen a man that night, who told him that his mother would be "coming to Him". She immediately thought she was going to die. "No," he said, "the man (Jesus) said you were going to walk with

78   Acts 5:15

Him." She immediately broke down and was saved. The backslidden father, seeing what Jesus had done, rededicated his life and became a committed Christian from that night. An estimated 30 people have joined their church as a direct result of the wonderful miracle that Jesus did in this little boy's life.

DAVID'S MIGHTY MEN WERE READY AND ARMED FOR THE WAR

"And these are the numbers of the bands that were ready armed to the war, and came to David to Hebron, to turn the kingdom of Saul to him, according to the word of the LORD." 1 Chronicles 12:23

God is equipping His Church with supernatural weaponry that transforms mindsets and opens the way for the Word of God to impact whole communities.

WEAPONS OF OUR WARFARE

"(For the weapons of our warfare are not carnal, but mighty through God to the pulling down of strong holds;) Casting down imaginations, and every high thing that exalteth itself against the knowledge of God, and bringing into captivity every thought to the obedience of Christ" 2 Corinthians 10:4-5

The Message Bible puts 2 Corinthians 10:4-5 this way:

"The tools of our trade aren't for marketing or manipulation, but they are for demolishing that entire massively corrupt culture. We use our powerful God-tools for smashing warped philosophies, tearing down barriers erected against the truth of God, fitting every loose thought and emotion and impulse into the structure of life shaped by Christ."

God has given us mighty, powerful, supernaturally-charged weapons that are geared to change mindsets, philosophies, cultures and the entire thinking of nations.

In the Bible the mindsets of individuals were dramatically transformed by one manifestation of the Holy Spirit.

The woman at the well had a total transformation when Jesus told her details of her marriages and relationship by the word of knowledge. The miracle caused the whole town to come out and hear Him.

The deliverance of the demoniac of the Gadarenes led to a total revival in the ten cities of Decapolis.

One touch of God's power saw Saul of Tarsus personally changed in his mind and philosophy. It also saw the whole world, from that time on, impacted in its thinking.

The following is an example of the impact of the operation of one of God's weapons. In this case, it was the operation of a word of knowledge.

One balmy Papua New Guinean night, I was preparing to preach in the National Stadium at Port Moresby.

I could see the glow of the stadium lights and my spirit stirred with holy anticipation. Tens of thousands of people streamed into the stadium as we anticipated a night of outstanding power demonstration.

Suddenly, I heard a knock on the door and the deep resonant voice of a Papua New Guinean man.

"Do you remember me?" he asked, as he sat down in my room.

He was impressively dressed in a grey pin-striped suit and carried an air of confidence. He asked if I remembered preaching a series of meetings at the Port Moresby University some years before. I recalled preaching to about 400 students at the University. It came to mind that half way through the message I had been stopped by the Lord with a sharp, accurate word of knowledge. I remember that I pointed to a section of the ground and described a young man's family background, people group, spiritual state and criminal activity in some detail, followed by an eternal challenge.

A young man who sat in line with my finger was a "Rascal" gang leader of a serious criminal group of young men whose situation God had given to me in great detail He was a gang leader by night and studied law by day. He had come, with a number of his gang members, to our meeting that night with a goal to totally disrupt and close it down. A sharp, detailed operation of God's weaponry, in the form of a word of knowledge, shafted into the meeting like a flash of lightning.

He fled to his dormitory and shook like a leaf. Finally convinced by one of his henchmen that I must have been informed of his details, he sheepishly returned.

At this point, some extraordinary miracles broke out in one section of the building. It was as though only one area, about 4.6 m by 4.6 m (15 feet by 15 feet), was under an open heaven. One after another, people shrieked, fell down and received extraordinary miracles in this small space. He explained to me that he had been gripped and frozen as he watched the manifestation of God explode in front of him.

For three days, he shook and struggled with what he had seen and heard. As he sat with me that night, he explained how after three days he threw open his heart to Christ. He went on to not only be a significant barrister but a powerful preacher that ministered to thousands of young people across his nation. From there, he continued to become significant in politics until he recently became Attorney General of his nation.

Truly, the weapons of our warfare are not natural but divinely powerful to absolutely changing mindsets, philosophies, speculations, humanistic unbelieving reasoning and godless imaginations. It is time for the Body of Christ to be fully armed for the task ahead in these last days.

A well-directed, supernatural word of knowledge, followed by a display of God's healing power, had dramatically swung the mindset of this man who is now impacting his nation for Christ.

Giant killers need ears tuned precisely to the voice of God.

GOD HAS OPENED HIS ARMOURY

"The LORD hath opened his armoury, and hath brought forth the weapons of his indignation: for this is the work of the Lord GOD of hosts in the land of the Chaldeans." Jeremiah 50:25

This is a real word for the Church today. The sin, depravity, injustice and rampant godlessness is like a plague across the Earth. Surely the indignation of God must have risen to a fever pitch. If ever He has opened His great supernatural armoury to His people it is now. This is the time for us to go with Him into the place of prayer and seek Him urgently. It is the time to go into His armoury and emerge with weaponry that will ruthlessly smash disease and devils and bring the convicting fire of the Throne Room.

God has thrown open the doors of His armoury to you and me. Let us spend time with Him learning to use His weaponry until, like David's mighty men, we can say we are armed for war with all the instruments of battle.

GIANT KILLERS ARE A SEPARATED PEOPLE

"And of the Gadites there separated themselves unto David into the hold to the wilderness..."
1 Chronicles 12:8a

Giant killers must know the secret place of separation with God, the place alone with Him where we are motivated, illuminated and empowered.

David's mighty men went alone with David to the cave in the wilderness, where they were trained, encouraged and prepared for war.

It is alone with God that we become sharp, as God hones us and intimately shares His presence and purpose with us. It was alone with God, in His awesome presence, that Moses received the detailed pattern for the Tabernacle. It was in the lonely, desolate hills of Tishbe in Gilead that Elijah was forged. It is in the place of intimacy, the separated place, that we will truly come to know Him. Daniel makes that clear:

> *"…but the people that do know their God shall be strong, and do exploits."* Daniel 11:32b

DAVID'S MIGHTY MEN HAD THE FACES OF LIONS

> *"…whose faces were like the faces of lions, and were as swift as the roes upon the mountains"* 1 Chronicles 12:8

Have you ever seen the look in a lion's eyes and the awesome appearance of the face of these extraordinary beasts? They are confident, resolved, certain of the power of their massive clawed paws and mighty teeth. Lions are confident in their powerfully muscled bodies, which are shaped to bring down their prey of any size. This is the look that comes on the face of people who know the awesome power of God that fills their entire being and the authority they carry in the spirit realm. This is the look that comes on the person of God's giant killers who view all opposition out of Hell as their "bread".

In the Vietnam War a phrase was coined: "the eye of the tiger". It was made famous with the "Rocky" movies. The title was given to men who had been wounded in battle and came back with a look in their eye of total fearless defiance. It was a look that comes out of the deep recesses of their souls. We are told in Scripture that the eye is the window that reveals the soul.

The face of the lion reflects an attitude of raw courage, stoic resistance and a conqueror's heart. Every one of God's giant killers will have these characteristics. God is raising an army of Holy Ghost warriors, with an overwhelming love and passion to redeem multitudes of people from the tyrannical grip of the arch enemy of men's souls. It's time for the lion's roar to echo like thunder out of the ranks of God's warriors.

SWIFT AS THE ROES UPON THE MOUNTAINS

"and were as swift as the roes upon the mountains"
1 Chronicles 12:8b

David's mighty men were fast and sure footed in the high places of the mountains. The Hebrew word swift *(mahar)*[79] means to flow like liquid, smooth and with the emphasis of speed.

Speed has always been a key to success in military campaigns. Alexander the Great could move his army like none had ever moved previously. His capacity to strike like a leopard was his trademark. The leopard, of all of Africa's big cats, can move with incredible stealth then strike from close range. The cheetah can run down its prey at 112.6 kilometres per hour (70 miles per hour). Shaka Zulu made his men discard their sandals and run barefoot for days. His army was one of the quickest in history.

Decisive thinking and speed to act have always given generals the advantage in battle.

David's mighty men were quick to move when they knew it was God's purpose. We are told that they moved with the ease of flowing water in the mountainous places.

The roe thrives in the high places, as did David's mighty men. God's plan for you and I is that we might move, confident and sure-footed, in the places where few people dare to venture. The high places are dangerous places where one slip can be deadly.

Giant killers have learned to move confidently in places where others fear to venture, to tread with confident quick steps reserved for the likes of Caleb, David and God's mighty men. God wants us to move with stability and ease as He takes us higher and leads us into situations that demand strong, secure and confident steps.

The roe (gazelle) is sure-footed in high rock mountain places. God's giant killer walks with stealth and confidence in the high places of success, achievement and the anointing of God. The high

[79]   Strong's H4116

places in ministry are places of added, even multiplied, pressure and temptation. In the thinner air concentration, integrity, confidence and purpose must be the steps of the giant killer. These are intuitive steps of confidence in God. A select few servants of God seem to negotiate and handle the daring steps set up for those who walk in the high places of impact for God.

GIANT KILLERS DON'T WAIT FOR PERFECT CONDITIONS

"These are they that went over Jordan in the first month, when it had overflown all his banks; and they put to flight all them of the valleys, both toward the east, and toward the west." 1 Chronicles 12:15

In the ancient world, warfare was seasonal. Armies fought when weather conditions were favourable. We read that David was still at his palace when kings go out to battle. Generally the winter months were not the time to manoeuvre armies. David's mighty men did not consider the conditions, only the timing and purpose of God.

It was not logical for an army to cross a heavily swollen river to go into battle. Fully armed in breastplate, helmet, shield and weaponry, it would seem suicidal for soldiers to cross a fast-flowing torrent. But these men were different. A raging torrent was simply a hurdle on their pathway of battle. Not only did they cross the river in full flood but proceeded to put to flight the enemy "of the valleys, both toward the east, and toward the west."[80]

David's mighty men did not consider circumstances. Three of David's men were prepared to break through Philistine lines to obtain a drink of water for their king from Bethlehem's well.[81]

Solomon declared,

"He that observeth the wind shall not sow; and he that regardeth the clouds shall not reap." Ecclesiastes 11:4

80   1 Chronicles 12:15
81   1 Chronicles 11:15-19

Giant killers don't wait for perfect conditions. They move with the direction of the Holy Ghost. Paul instructed Timothy to:

> *"Preach the word; be instant in season, out of season; reprove, rebuke, exhort with all longsuffering and doctrine."* 2 Timothy 4:2

In Genesis 26, God instructed Isaac to sow in the middle of a great famine. Any farmer will tell you that this is the wrong time to sow, but Isaac stepped out on God's direction and reaped a massive harvest that took him into a place of enormous wealth.

Here then is God's great challenge to his giant killers - to trust God and to:

> *"...lean not unto thine own understanding."*
> Proverbs 3:5

Alexander the Great used unfavourable conditions to his own advantage. He took advantage of the logical thinking of his opponents and do the opposite to spring stunning surprises on his enemies. No swollen river was seen as an obstacle and any terrain could be made to work to his advantage.

As giant killers, we must move in obedience and God's timing regardless of the conditions we confront.

GIANT KILLERS UNDERSTAND TIMES AND SEASONS

> *"And of the children of Issachar, which were men that had understanding of the times, to know what Israel ought to do; the heads of them were two hundred; and all their brethren were at their commandment."*
> 1 Chronicles 12:32

David's mighty men had gained powerfully from his influence.

This group of mighty men had "understanding" of the times. The Hebrew word for understanding "biyn"[82] means insight, prudence, and intelligence. Daniel had "biyn" on any topic, which Nebuchadnezzar desired. Giant killers need an insight, understanding or an "uncanny sense" of what is occurring in events around them, to know when and what moves to make. Great results for God generally occur when a person moves with God-given understanding and timing in His purposes.

When the Philistines came against David after his coronation, before going into battle, he "enquired of God".[83]

> "...Shall I go up against the Philistines? and wilt thou deliver them into mine hand?..." 1 Chronicles 14:10

God gave him direction and great victory occurred. When they came again, David enquired a second time. God gave him clear direction as to timing and method, which led to further great success.

We learn from David and his mighty men the absolute significance of a listening ear. Therefore, we understand the keys to success in our times and have a clear understanding of the methods needed to achieve great things. It is significant that the dedication of priests in the Old Testament involved blood and oil applied to the big toe, thumb and ear. What a picture for us that shows an anointed listening ear to times and methods, anointed hands knowing what to do and anointed feet knowing where to go.

As an evangelist, I want to know where to go, which places are ripe for the taking and who to align with in conquest. I want to know the key things to preach that will open up the environment to the power of God. I want my ear tuned to hear words of knowledge and the things that God has planned in advance.

Two weeks ago, we spoke at a large conference in the beautiful country of Samoa in the South Pacific.

As I drove around the magnificent tropical island seeking God, I was

82   Strong's H995
83   1 Chronicles 14:10

desperate to know what God wanted to do that night. I was uncertain what message to preach and, as I prayed, all that came through my spirit was, "The deaf. The deaf." I knew at that time what God was going to do that night.

As a preacher, I like to pray for much of the day leading up to the night meeting, "What do you want to do Lord? Where will the sick be? What are their conditions?" After four or so hours praying this way, I begin to live the night meeting before I arrive. I want to know the times and the season.

That night in Samoa, I preached a short faith-building word then called for people to bring the deaf and the dumb. One after another, the deaf ears popped open then those of the deaf and mute. Some 15 deaf ears had opened then those of several deaf mutes. I don't think we missed seeing one of them healed that night.

If we seek Him, He will reveal to us the times and give us clear understanding of how to move.

AGE IS NOT A PRE-REQUISITE TO VALOUR

"And Zadok, a young man mighty of valour, and of his father's house twenty and two captains."
1 Chronicles 12:28

Age is not a guide to human courage and resolve, as we have seen with Caleb and Joshua. Among David's mighty men were young men. I have previously mentioned that the first recorded giant killer, Moses, was over 100-years-old when the first victory occurred over Og of Bashan. The next two giant killers, Joshua and Caleb, were over 85-years-old, while the next was David, a teenage boy. Zadok, one of David's mighty men, was a young valiant man set over some 22 captains. If each captain was set over at least one hundred men or as many as 1000 men, we can calculate that the minimum number of men set under this young man of war was a minimum 2,200 men and as many as 22,000 men.

"And Zadok, a young man mighty of valour..."
1 Chronicles 12:28

This young man was set over some 22 captains (warrior chiefs) of his father's house.

Young Zadoks all over the world are being raised up.

The mighty Welsh Revival, the impact of which touched the whole earth, exploded in the first decade of the 20th Century under the hand of a young miner in his mid-20s, Evan Roberts. He carried such a tangible, convicting and powerful anointing of God that the whole of Wales was gripped and shaken in a few years. The revival that saw 70,000 converts in the first month was carried by teams of unknown young men and women who were mainly in their 20s. Even the newspapers recorded that the whole nation was engulfed, "by an unseen power that showed no sign of lifting its hand".

As a young man in his 20s, the great preacher, Charles Spurgeon, had thousands of people in his church.

One of my favourite churches, which I have preached in over many years, is Christian City Church in Oxford Falls, Sydney. Young men from the church have for years enthusiastically sought me out to see what miracles we have been seeing in our crusade meetings. Now I ask them, "What are you guys seeing?"

One of the young men who is full of God, a Zadok, a valiant young warrior, came to me so excited that I thought he would burst. He explained that he had been at work when he heard a terrible noise like an explosion outside. On the road outside of the building, a vehicle had slammed into a tree. The car was a wreck, with the tree embedded near to the windscreen. Paramedics were already on the scene. Inside the vehicle, a man was crushed against the steering wheel, his knees under his chin, his skull wide open and obviously dead. My friend moved towards the car, as paramedics stood with the awareness of another road statistic.

This young "Zadok", like a military commander, declared, "I am a man of God. Please let me pray." They agreed and he cried out for life to return to the unfortunate man. He was cut out of the wreck alive and left hospital a few days later with a stitched head and his leg in plaster. How inspiring to see young "Zadoks" and "Zadokettes" demonstrating Kingdom power, stepping out to pioneer churches and going to the nations to touch the multitudes for Christ.

DAVID'S MIGHTY GIANT KILLERS WERE GENEROUS

"Moreover they that were nigh them, even unto Issachar and Zebulun and Naphtali, brought bread on asses, and on camels, and on mules, and on oxen, and meat, meal, cakes of figs, and bunches of raisins, and wine, and oil, and oxen, and sheep abundantly: for there was joy in Israel." 1 Chronicles 12:40

These mighty men were generous. They came and gave abundantly into the campaign. They came with the basics of bread in great proportion. They also brought luxury items of food and wine, including beef and mutton. They supplied with great effort and brought joy and great morale into the camp.

It is interesting to note the two tribal groups who are recorded for their generosity, Issachar Zebulun and Napthali. Jacob leaning on his staff, near death, prophesied over these tribes.

"Issachar is a strong ass couching down between two burdens: And he saw that rest was good, and the land that it was pleasant; and bowed his shoulder to bear, and became a servant unto tribute." Genesis 49:14-15

These men of Issachar were burden-bearers, servants willing to bend their backs to carry the load. There are giant killers in the Body of Christ, people whose servanthood and generosity flood the army of God with zeal and joyous morale in the midst of battle. The quiet achievers, who do not seek accolades but simply wish to share the load, are so vital and significant in the Kingdom. These are the people who baulk at no task and passionately wish to see the Church advance. They will take up the dirty jobs and do the tasks that others avoid.

I heard the testimony of a Christian man with perhaps the most boring job possible. Working on a motor vehicle production line, some years ago, his task was simply to put hub caps on the vehicles. The hubcaps clipped onto the wheel with a gentle hit. Day after day he smiled and rejoiced as he "thumped" on the hub caps. His joy was that he was working as unto the Lord and was also placing a simple gospel tract inside every one. These would later fall out and be read each time a tyre had to be changed or a wheel checked.

Thank God for the Christians who will rejoice in simple tasks and will be burden-bearers behind the scenes, generous in their desire to see the Kingdom advance.

> *"Zebulun shall dwell at the haven of the sea; and he shall be for an haven of ships; and his border shall be unto Zidon."* Genesis 49:13

This speaks of one who gives hospitality and creates a place of peace and comfort to those who are in the midst of storms.

Zebulun speaks to us of the people who open their homes to strangers and spend time with the rejected and unwanted people. Zebulun speaks to us of those who wish to make their lives a haven to people smashed and ravaged by the violent, tempestuous storms of life.

> *"Naphtali is a hind let loose: he giveth goodly words."*
> Genesis 49:21

Here is the encourager, the giver of life-filled words. These are the people in the Body of Christ who inspire, motivate, encourage and build confidence and strength into the hearts of God's giant killers.

In Judges 5, Deborah describes the tribes of Issachar, Zebulun and Naphtali in the great battle with Sisera. Issachar were alongside Deborah in the valley (hard place) while:

> *"Zebulun and Naphtali were a people that jeopardized their lives unto the death in the high places of the field."*
> Judges 5:18

These tribes had a reputation for servanthood, valour of the highest form and extreme generosity. Over many years of evangelism to the nations, we were supported by one of Australia's most famous artists the late Pro Hart. His great generosity allowed us to finance huge outdoor campaigns with tens of thousands of decisions for Christ. I'm sure he has been shown in Heaven the great number of souls that have been won for Christ through his willingness to bring large amounts of finance into the Kingdom.

How the great giant killing campaign in which we are involved needs the Zebuluns, Naphtalis and Issachars to bring an abundance of supplies and finance, together with sustenance, to lift morale and release the valiant men and women to their great call and task.

DAVID'S MIGHTY MEN CONCLUSION

David's mighty men were used of God to eradicate the remaining giants upon the earth. A study of their characteristics give us a picture of the character required for today's giant killers. Let's take a final look at them:

1. They were all men of valour – mighty men of war.
2. They were equipped with all the instruments of warfare.[84]
3. They separated themselves to David for training and preparation.[85]

---

84   1 Chronicles 12:2, 8, 24, 33, 38.
85   1 Chronicles 12:8

4. They had the confident appearance of lions.[86]

5. They were quick to move, like gazelles on the high mountains.[87]

6. They didn't wait for the seasons and circumstances to be perfect.[88]

7. Age was not a pre-requisite to impact in battle.[89]

8. They understood the times and how to move.[90]

9. They were single-minded.[91]

10. They could keep rank and move.[92]

11. They were people of great generosity.[93]

When we look at the characteristics of the giant killers of Scripture, it is impossible not to be challenged and stirred.

As I read of these lives, I understand that the giants certainly did their homework for them and clarified their place with God as they sought out the warrior within them.

Giants will come against every one of us whose passion is to serve God. World events and growing stresses, economic, political and religious, point out that the years to come will be filled with the onslaught of a host of giants raised up to harass, hinder and restrict everything that God has planned to do.

A generation of giant killing warriors whose attitude is akin to those we've studied is being raised across the earth in preparation for the Church's greatest day.

---

86   1 Chronicles 12:8

87   1 Chronicles 12:8

88   1 Chronicles 12:15

89   1 Chronicles 12:28

90   1 Chronicles 12:32

91   1 Chronicles 12:33, 38

92   1 Chronicles 12:33, 38.

93   1 Chronicles 12:40

7

JESUS

THE ULTIMATE GIANT KILLER

"And having spoiled principalities and powers, he made a shew of them openly, triumphing over them in it."
Colossians 2:15

The great giant of the ages, prince of the underworld, the hater of God and enemy of the human race, stalked the Earth clutching in his hands the keys of Hell and Death. Legal dominion had been placed into his hands as ruler of the cosmos.[1] His vicious, malevolent, hissing orders sent his hordes across the earth on errands of savage destruction. The whole human race groaned under his tyrannical regime.

Who could stand against him as he flaunted his position of power across the earth? God's delegated authority had been passed to him from Adam. Satan sought to bring mankind into total submission to himself. What could be done to bring him down? No ordinary man could bring down this giant.

The giant prince of the cosmos could only be brought down by God Himself. God always has His Man.

We have read of Moses, Joshua, Caleb and David but God Himself <u>came to the Earth</u> and took the form of a Man. He is a Man who took

1   www.dictionary.com
Origin: 1150–1200; ME < Greek cósmos order, form, arrangement, the world or universe

upon Himself the sin of the world and then crushed the great giant, stripping his power, then paraded His enemy and his hordes in a universal display of total dominion.

All of the giant killers we have studied are a type of the One who gave them their greatness. All of their incredible exploits point to the One who faced the giants of Death and Hell and the great giant, Satan, whose chilling defiance has challenged all of God's creation. Like the Philistine god Dagon, prostrate before the Ark of God, his head severed and hands broken off, and Goliath of Gath face down on the earth, his head severed by David and his sword taken, so Satan crashed prostrate at the feet of Christ, his head crushed and the keys of Hell and death stripped from his grasp.

Moses descended from the fire of God's glory to face the awesome giants ahead. Jesus stepped out of His eternal position, in the fiery glory and authority of the Throne Room of God, took the form of a Man whose purpose was to utterly destroy the evil one, the great giant, Satan and his foul hordes.

Joshua mentored, as a son, by Moses cut a swath through the giants of the Promised Land as the anointed General of Israel. After encountering the "Captain of his Salvation", Joshua went forth as an unstoppable champion. The name Joshua is well translated as Jesus ("Jehovah Saviour"). Joshua, a type of Christ, was led through the Promised Land by Jesus the Captain of his Salvation. Today the Great Captain of your salvation is ready to lead you into your destiny as you cut a swath through the giants that in any way will seek to slow your progress.

Caleb sought for his mountain and no matter what opposed him, he seized it and brought down the giants and the strongholds, which opened the way for the people of God. Jesus also saw a mountain to be seized. He had seen it before the foundation of the earth. It was a mountain of horror, pain and blood. It was the terrifying mountain of Golgotha where Satan defiantly seemed to rule. Like Caleb of old, Jesus set his "face like a flint"[2] to go and seize our destiny. For the joy set before Him, the eternal destiny to be claimed, He faced the horrendous mountain.

2   Isaiah 50:7

227

"...endured the cross, despising the shame, and is set down at the right hand of the throne of God."
Hebrews 12:2

At the mountain of Golgotha, Jesus faced every giant that Hell could conjure. He faced tormenting, ridiculing, taunting giants of horrendous agony, rejection, mockery, isolation, doubt, fear and every foul thing that could be imagined. They taunted him like Goliath of old and shouted into his face on this miserable demon-possessed mountain of horror. But should the princes of this world have had one glimpse of the subsequent events they never would have confronted the Ultimate Giant Killer.

After Jesus paid the price of sin for the whole world, He stepped down into the portals of Hell. Satan, like Dagon and Goliath, found himself face down before the One who trod alone the winepress of the fierce wrath of Almighty God. The eternal fury was directed with unbridled crushing power at the dark giant of Hell.

The Seed of the woman, raised His foot and crushed the serpent's head, stripped him of his power and tore away the keys of Hell and Death. Rising triumphantly from the dead, He led captivity captive, released the souls held captive and triumphantly declared,

*"All power is given unto me in heaven and in earth.
Go ye therefore..."* Matthew 28:18-19

David was a shepherd boy from an obscure place called Bethlehem. What a place for a giant killer to be born. Significantly, God chose this simple place for the Great Giant Killer, Jesus, to be born. Shepherds from the same hills where David was trained as a shepherd warrior, came to see the new King.

Like David, Jesus was rejected by his family and was one from whom men turned their faces (Isaiah 53:3).

Goliath's crash down before the stunned armies is a great type of Satan's crushing defeat, as his host of demons and God's heavenly host of angels watched in stunned amazement.

As David walked off the battlefield carrying Goliath's head, he made a direct line to Jerusalem. All about him the multitudes roared their approval, screaming with delight as he paraded his trophy of dominion before friend and foe alike. Having "spoiled" Goliath he made a spectacle in Jerusalem, which was a place held by Jebusites ("polluters of that which is holy"). How his enemies must have cringed and feared and sensed their impending demise. David soon came and made this city his stronghold.

In the same way, Jesus, "having spoiled principalities and powers,... made a shew of them openly, triumphing over them in it".[3] He spelt out to the whole world His victory and the fact that he would be coming back to make the whole earth His stronghold.

David's Mighty Men are a great picture of us. They became men just like David, who had the courage of David, his skill, his capacity for war and the same results. These giant killers were forged under David's mighty anointing and became equally triumphant in battle.

This is a picture of the disciples of Christ. They also become mighty, unstoppable giant killers. It was said of Peter and John that, as people watched their boldness and the evident miracle power that they carried, they were just like Jesus.

As we have seen the raw courage, boldness, unstoppable attitude and skill in battle of the great giant killing warriors of history we see the characteristics that we must emulate and follow. This will change us.

However, the greater truth is this: The great Giant Killer of history has actually come to indwell us, to fill us with His own mighty power, and has given us all authority in His name to confront, and stand in total triumph against, every giant before us. The supreme Giant Killer of the age has filled us "with all the fullness of God", "and hast made us unto our God kings and priests: and we shall reign on the earth."[4]

He has informed us that "no weapon that is formed against"[5] us will have effect and that every voice raised against us we will silence. This is our heritage.

---

3   Colossians 2:15
4   Revelation 5:10
5   Isaiah 54:17

Rise up, giant killer, you who have been saved and filled with the unlimited, unstoppable power of the Eternal King of the Universe. Rise up, you sharp implement in the hand of God and recognise that you have been chosen by God for this great moment in world history to destroy giants, seize mountains and impact whole nations.

You are God's unstoppable giant killer. The giants you face are truly:

"The Breakfast of Champions."

AUTHOR BIOGRAPHY

Tim Hall is a dynamic preacher whose emphasis on miracles, signs and wonders is impacting on the church globally. He is one of Australia's best known and well-loved evangelists conducting miracle campaigns, conferences and citywide healing rallies throughout the world with crowds up to 100,000 in attendance.

He is the founder of Tim Hall International Ministries Inc. and has pioneered and pastored churches across Australia. He is married to Jacquelyn and lives in Adelaide, South Australia.

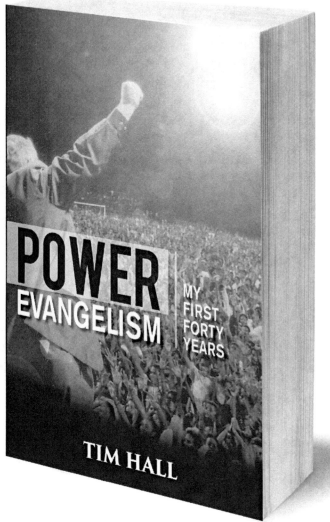

CPSIA information can be obtained
at www.ICGtesting.com
Printed in the USA
FSOW02n1736270417
33476FS